Written by
June Hetzel, Ph.D., and Deborah McIntire, M.A.

Contributing Writers
Sandy Gardner
Michelle L. Pecanic

Editor: Teri L. Fisch
Illustrator: Kate Flanagan
Cover Illustrator: David Willardson
Designer/Production: Moonhee Pak/Carrie Carter
Cover Designer: Moonhee Pak
Art Director: Tom Cochrane
Project Director: Carolea Williams

Table of Contents

Introduction

Successful writers identify themselves as authors with legitimate voices capable of expressing valuable messages. The lessons in *Steps to Writing Success: Level 1* are designed to help you guide your students towards viewing themselves as authors and taking ownership of their writing. Use the real-world ideas in this book to encourage students to develop a respect for writing, take pride in their work, and become self-reflective, lifelong writers. Enhance this process by providing opportunities for students to read their stories aloud to their classmates in an Author's Chair, publish their stories in class anthologies or weekly newsletters, and share their stories with other students within the school. The lessons in this book teach skills that are commonly found in most language arts standards. Refer to the Scope and Sequence on page 7 to link lessons to the language arts standards your school, district, or state requires.

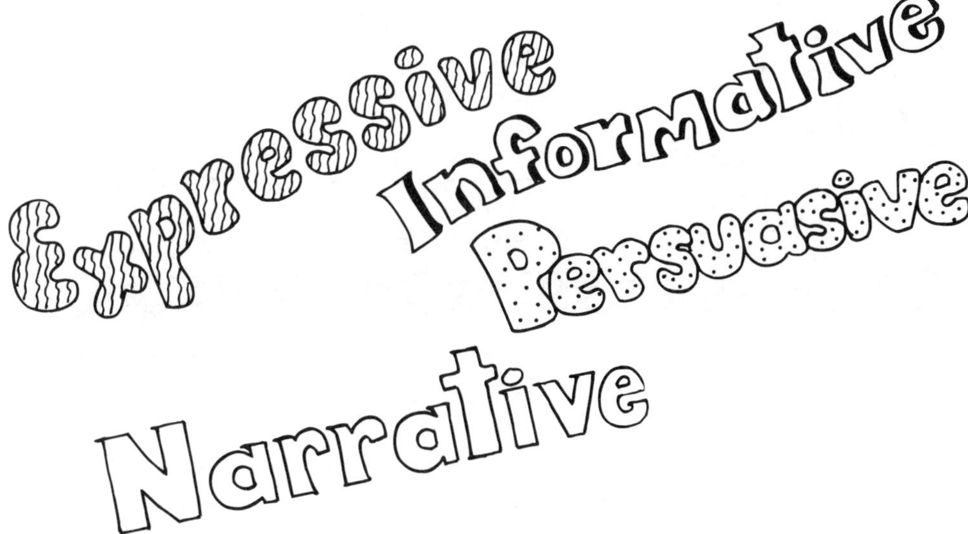

The 28 lessons in *Steps to Writing Success: Level 1* explore the four domains of writing: expressive, narrative, informative, and persuasive. In **expressive writing,** students learn to become better observers and writers as they use sensory detail, alliteration, and strong verbs to describe their thoughts. In **narrative writing,** students learn to tell a story by developing characters, setting, problem, solution, and dialogue. In **informative writing,** students learn to organize factual information in an understandable fashion. In **persuasive writing,** students learn to organize their thoughts and beliefs about familiar subjects.

Use the lessons in this resource to teach students how to create a variety of writing products that reflect all four writing domains—an important skill that students rarely practice in the elementary grades. Students will learn to use the writing process to effectively write several sentences about one topic. This book is designed to encourage students to extend their writing beyond stories, to writing they can apply to real-life situations and experiences. Encourage students to publish each piece of writing in a creative manner. Suggestions for publishing are included in the Presentation section of each lesson. In addition, the writing templates at the end of the book provide students with fun paper to publish their work. You will be amazed at how your students' writing abilities and confidence soar as they experience success in writing across the four domains.

Overview of the Writing Process

The writing process occurs in five stages: prewriting, drafting, revising, editing, and publishing.

Prewriting involves a structured brainstorming session meant to elicit spontaneous thinking about a specific topic. This stage occurs before formal writing. Students generally record and arrange the ideas or information generated during prewriting on a graphic organizer. As students are beginning to learn to write, invite the class to brainstorm word banks and lists for the subject they will be writing about. Post them in the room for students to access as an easy reference.

The **rough draft** is the second stage, but it is actually the "first round" of writing. During this stage, encourage students to write spontaneously about the information on the graphic organizer. Students should not be overly concerned with spelling at this stage, although their writing does need to be readable.

During the **revising** stage, have students with advanced writing capabilities evaluate their writing on four levels: entire piece, paragraph or stanza, sentence or line, and word. Ask students to carefully consider the "big picture" as they rearrange or revise text to clarify meaning. They should also review their work to make sure it satisfies the requirements of the writing lesson (as defined by the corresponding rubric). Revising is often overwhelming for beginning writers. They may begin by only looking at individual words and sentences to replace a word here or there. Encourage them to continue to do so until they are ready to revise at a larger level. Provide an opportunity for students to give and receive feedback during a "read around." Have students sit in a circle and, on your cue, pass their paper to the right until each student has read three to five different papers and written suggestions for revisions on the back of each paper. You will notice an increase in the quality of students' writing when they incorporate peer feedback.

After students revise their papers, they are ready for **editing.** This stage involves checking for correct spelling, punctuation, capitalization, and sentence structure. Ask students to focus on the composition of sentences to make sure they are grammatically correct, are not missing words, and do not contain extraneous words. Encourage students to use the rubric on page 9 to edit their work. Enhance the editing process by using the teacher rubric on page 8 to evaluate each student's writing.

After the editing stage is complete, students move into **publishing** their work as a final draft. This is often the most rewarding stage for students because it is at this point that writers can finally see their completed work in a polished form and can share it with their classmates.

A Note about Spelling

Students should not focus on spelling during the initial draft and revision stages of their writing. Ask them to focus only on clearly communicating their ideas. However, once the ideas are refined, correct spelling is critical so the audience can enjoy the writing. Unfortunately, students regularly struggle with spelling. Use the following ideas to address spelling during the writing process:

- Sticky Notes: Walk around the room with sticky notes as students are writing. When students ask how to spell a word, quickly write it on a sticky note and place the note on their desk.
- Try It Cards: Give each student a stack of index cards held together with a metal ring. Instead of telling students to raise their hand when they need help with a word, ask them to simply write a "best guess" for the spelling on a "Try It Card." Verify or correct each student's spellings as you walk around the room.

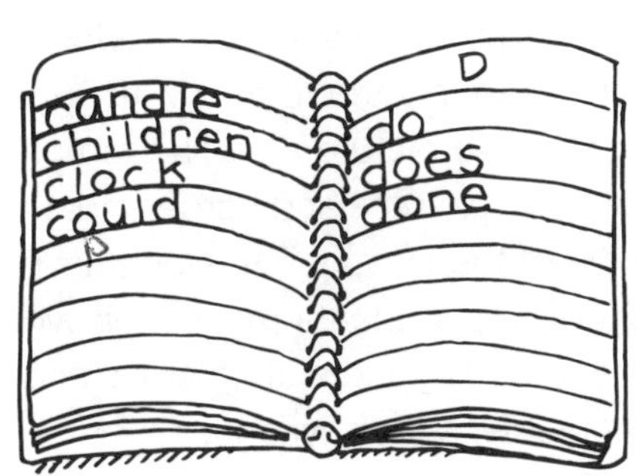

- Personalized Dictionaries: A personalized dictionary can simply be a spiral binder. Have students label every other page with a letter of the alphabet and record words that stumped them in the spelling process. Over time, students will collect important writing words and create a ready reference tool. Encourage students to look up hard-to-spell words in a published dictionary such as *Scholastic Children's Dictionary* (Scholastic) and add correct spellings to their personalized dictionary for easy reference.
- Word Walls: Word walls meet the collective spelling needs of a classroom. To make a word wall, post the alphabet on the classroom wall, write key spelling and vocabulary words on index cards, and display each card beneath the letter of the alphabet that matches the first letter of the word. Continue to remove and add words as needed throughout the school year.
- Sight Word Lists: Every student needs access to the words most commonly used in writing. Generally, students use sight word lists (e.g., Dolch or Fry). Systematic study of high-frequency words can only benefit young writers. Highlight these words in personalized dictionaries or on word walls.

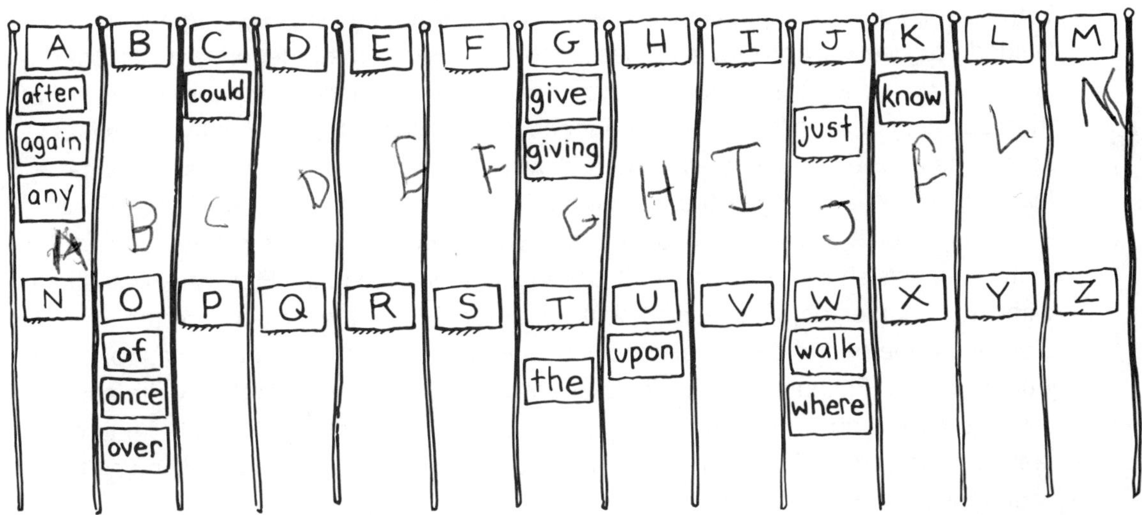

Lesson Overview

Steps to Writing Success: Level 1 features easy-to-follow, comprehensive lesson plans for helping students complete 28 writing projects, with seven lessons focusing on each of the domains: expressive, narrative, informative, and persuasive. Each lesson lists the objective and critical components of the writing project and includes detailed directions for preparing all the required materials and preliminary activities that will engage students' interest and build their background knowledge. (Typical classroom materials such as scissors, crayons, markers, glue, and writing paper and materials needed for the Presentation ideas are not listed in the Preparation section.) Each lesson also provides explicit steps for direct instruction, guided practice, and independent practice; suggested ways for students to present their writing projects; teaching tips; and cross-curricular student activities. Each lesson features a "word recognition" reproducible to help students identify vocabulary related to the writing topic. All the lessons also feature a writing template or shape book with pictures and borders that relate to the theme of the lesson. The student rubric on page 9 will help students focus their writing, develop their revision and editing skills, and be more accountable in their writing.

Preceding Week

- Preparation
  - ✔ Read aloud books
  - ✔ Gather materials
  - ✔ Photocopy reproducibles
  - ✔ Make transparencies

Day 1

- Setting the Stage
- Instructional Input

Day 2

- Guided Practice
- Independent Practice
  - ✔ Hand out student rubric

Days 3–5

- Independent Practice continues
- Presentation
- Assign journal prompts

Each lesson in *Steps to Writing Success: Level 1* should be taught within three to five days. Prepare for each lesson by reviewing the Preparation section during the preceding week. Read aloud the books listed or others with similar content to introduce students to the topic that will be the focus of the writing lesson. Picture books help students at every level quickly and clearly identify the elements of good writing. Set up comfortable areas with pillows, beanbag chairs, and carpet pieces to create a relaxed and enjoyable environment. On the first day of the lesson, implement the activities from the Setting the Stage section, and then proceed with the Instructional Input activity that follows. On the second day, begin the Guided Practice activity with your class, and then assign the Independent Practice activity. Two rubrics are included in this book. Fill in the critical components—listed at the beginning of each lesson—on the teacher rubric (page 8), and photocopy a class set to use as you evaluate your students' writing. Give students a student rubric (page 9) at the beginning of the Independent Practice activity so they are aware of the requirements of the writing project and your expectations before they begin to write. Students should complete the Independent Practice and the Presentation sections within two to three days, depending on the requirements of the project. Use the prompts at the end of the list of Teaching Hints/Extensions to provide ideas for daily journal writing. Encourage students to count the number of words they write each day, and have them record this data on a graph for self-feedback. Your students will feel a strong sense of accomplishment and be motivated to continue writing as they watch the number of words on their graphs grow.

Scope and Sequence

The skills listed on the chart represent those commonly found in most language arts standards.

Lesson Title	Complete Sentences	Supporting Details	Capitalization	Quotation Marks	Ending Punctuation	Sequencing	Category
Touch and Feel	•	•	•		•		Expressive
Awesome Animals	•	•	•		•		Expressive
Tasty Treats	•	•	•		•		Expressive
I Spy		•	•				Expressive
Rhyme Time	•	•	•		•		Expressive
Animal Antics	•	•	•		•		Expressive
What's My Sound?	•	•	•		•		Expressive
Bunny Tales	•	•	•		•	•	Narrative
Kangaroo Chaos	•	•	•		•	•	Narrative
Billy the Bear	•	•	•	•	•	•	Narrative
A Whale of a Tale	•	•	•	•	•	•	Narrative
Lionnel the Lion	•	•	•	•	•	•	Narrative
Monkey Business	•	•	•	•	•	•	Narrative
Creative Crocodile	•	•	•	•	•	•	Narrative
Hot Topic	•	•	•		•	•	Informative
Cars, Buildings, People	•	•	•		•	•	Informative
Down Under	•	•	•		•	•	Informative
Back to Nature	•	•	•		•	•	Informative
E-I-E-I-O	•	•	•		•	•	Informative
Green, Green Everywhere	•	•	•		•	•	Informative
It's Cold	•	•	•		•	•	Informative
All-Stars	•	•	•		•	•	Persuasive
Let's Celebrate	•	•	•		•	•	Persuasive
Rainbow Writing	•	•	•		•	•	Persuasive
On the Move	•	•	•		•	•	Persuasive
Helping Hands	•	•	•		•	•	Persuasive
Yummy	•	•	•		•	•	Persuasive
Playtime	•	•	•		•	•	Persuasive

Student's Name ______________________ Date ______________________

Writing Assignment ______________________

Teacher Rubric

	☹	😐	☺
Critical Components			
Each sentence begins with a capital letter.			
Each sentence ends with the correct punctuation.			
Mechanics			
Did the student capitalize proper nouns?			
Did the student write complete sentences?			
Did the student write grammatically correct sentences?			
Did the student correctly spell common words and words related to this lesson?			

The student did a good job ____

____.

An area of growth I see is ____

____.

An area to improve is ____

____.

Name ______________________________ Date ______________________

Topic ______________________________

Student Rubric

	☹	😐	☺
Did I begin each sentence with a capital letter?			
Did I end each sentence with the correct punctuation?			
Did I write complete sentences?			
Did I spell words correctly?			

I like ____

____.

I don't like ____

____.

An area to improve is ____

____.

Touch and Feel

Preparation

Read aloud books about the sense of touch.

- *Feeling Things* by Allen Fowler (Children's Press)
- *The Sweet Touch* by Lorna Balian (Humbug Books)
- *Touching* by Helen Frost (Capstone Press)

Collect objects with a variety of textures (e.g., rough—sandpaper, smooth—silk, squishy—sponge, bumpy—popcorn, rubbery—balloon). Place them in a bag.

Gather a plastic bag, a cotton ball, a pebble, and a balloon for each student and two pieces of chart paper.

Make copies of these reproducibles.
- Touch Word Recognition (page 13) transparency, class set of photocopies
- Texture Booklet (page 14) transparency, class set of photocopies
- rubric (page 9) class set of photocopies

Setting the Stage

Show students the "mystery bag" of objects. Pull out one object at a time, and place it on a table. Invite students to name the object and share what they know about it. Then, have students feel each object and list words that describe its texture. Record the words on a piece of chart paper. Brainstorm with the class additional words that describe texture, such as *rough, smooth, squishy, bumpy, rubbery, silky, prickly,* and *sticky,* and record them on the chart paper. Review the words by reading them and having students repeat the words after you. Then, have the class chorally read the list of words.

OBJECTIVE

The student will write simple sentences that describe the texture of three objects.

CRITICAL COMPONENTS

- Sensory detail words are used to describe the texture of objects.
- Each sentence begins with a capital letter.
- Each sentence ends with the correct punctuation.

Instructional Input

1 Place the objects from Setting the Stage on a table or desk. Review the word list from Setting the Stage. Say a word, and invite a volunteer to use a pointer to identify the word and pick out an object with the same texture. Have the student say a sentence in which he or she identifies the object and its texture. Encourage the student to say a second sentence in which he or she identifies the object and another word that describes its texture. For example, the student might say *This sponge is squishy. This sponge is also soft.* Add any new "texture words" to the list.

2 Give each student a plastic bag. Invite students to go on a scavenger hunt in the classroom to find and collect objects with the textures on the list. You may have to place objects in the classroom if you don't have objects with different textures in the room. For example, place a bowl of popcorn (rough or bumpy texture) or a jar of cotton balls (soft texture) in the room.

3 When students complete the scavenger hunt, invite them to describe their findings by identifying each object and its texture. For example, a student might say *The marble I found is smooth.* Record their sentences on a second piece of chart paper.

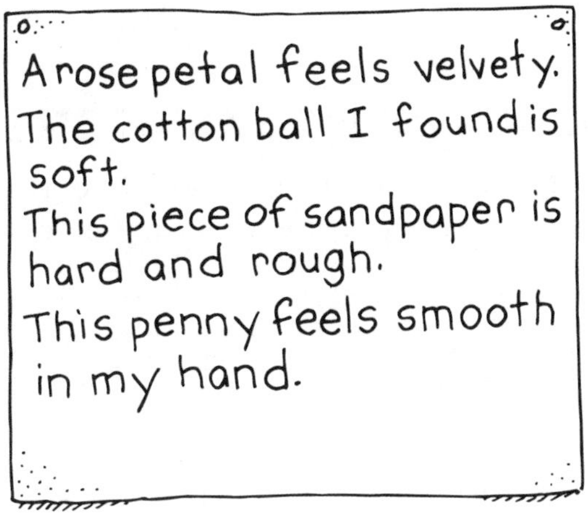

A rose petal feels velvety.
The cotton ball I found is soft.
This piece of sandpaper is hard and rough.
This penny feels smooth in my hand.

Guided Practice

1 Give each student a Touch Word Recognition reproducible. Invite volunteers to identify the picture in each box. Read aloud each set of words, and then use the words to complete a sentence frame. For example, say *Ice cream is hot. Ice cream is cold. Ice cream is sticky.* Tell students to fill in the bubble next to the word that best describes the texture of the picture.

2 Display the Touch Word Recognition overhead transparency. Review the correct answers, and have students circle them.

3 Write on the board or on a sentence strip *A _____ feels ______.* Give each student a cotton ball, a pebble, and a balloon. Display the Texture Booklet overhead transparency. Place a cotton ball in the first box on the transparency. Ask students to help you write about how the item feels by completing the sentence frame. Record the sentence frame and several responses from students on the transparency. Repeat this process with the pebble and the balloon.

Independent Practice

1 Give each student three objects, or invite students to use the objects from the scavenger hunt or find other small objects outside. Tell students that they can create their own sentences or use the sentence frame to write sentences that describe the objects.

2 Have students revise and edit their rough draft and then use the rubric to evaluate their writing.

Presentation

- Have students **publish** their final drafts on the Texture Booklet reproducibles. Then, have them glue or tape their objects in the boxes, cut on the dotted lines, and staple the pages together.
- Encourage students to **share** their books. Reinforce correct vocabulary usage.
- **Display** students' books in a basket in the classroom library.

TEACHING HINTS/EXTENSIONS

- Make a word wall for texture words. Invite students to join in the fun by adding more words under each heading. Use the following example as a guide.

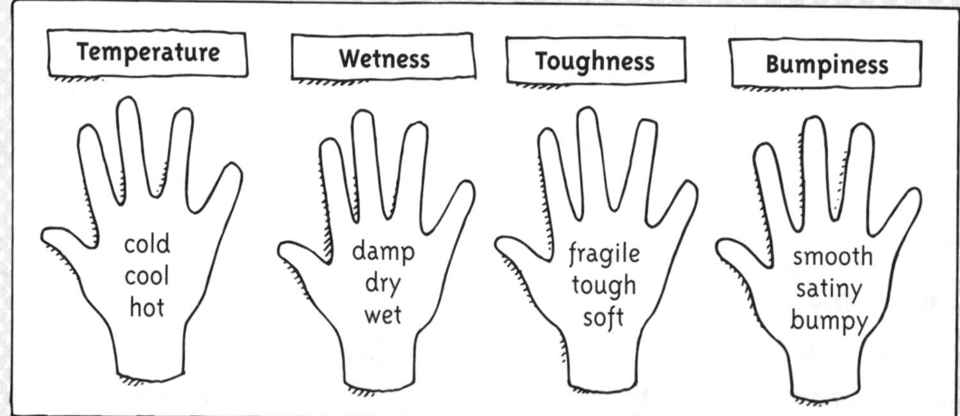

- Students love sharing time. Invite each student to bring a bag with a "mystery object" in it. Have a volunteer reach in the bag and use texture words to describe the object. Invite the rest of the class to identify the object.
- Hand out objects and large word cards with texture words written on them. Invite students to match the correct texture card with each object.
- Have students complete one or more of these writing prompts in a journal:
  - ✔ Describe how popcorn feels.
  - ✔ Describe how the bark of a tree feels.
  - ✔ Describe how a baseball glove feels.

Name Michelle Date 10/28/06

Touch Word Recognition

Directions: Fill in the bubble next to the word that best describes the picture.

○ hot ● cold ○ sticky	● velvety ○ rough ○ hard
○ cold ○ hard ● rubbery	● hot ○ cold ○ hard
● soft ○ sticky ○ rubbery	● rough ○ rubbery ○ cold
● sticky ○ soft ○ hard	○ smooth ● prickly ○ hot

Texture Booklet

By ______________________________

Glue or tape object here.

Glue or tape object here.

Glue or tape object here.

Awesome Animals

Preparation

Read aloud books that include alliteration.

- *A My Name is Alice* by Jane Bayer (Dutton)
- *Aster Aardvark's Alphabet Adventures* by Steven Kellogg (Econo-Clad Books)
- *Busy Buzzing Bumblebees and Other Tongue Twisters* by Alvin Schwartz (HarperCollins)

Gather a large sheet of construction paper and a magazine for each student.

Obtain a copy of *Animalia* by Graeme Base (Abrams Books).

Write each letter of the alphabet on two or three index cards.

Make copies of these reproducibles.

- Animal Word Recognition (page 18) transparency, class set of photocopies
- Amazing Animals (page 19) transparency, class set of photocopies
- Awesome Animals (page 20) class set of photocopies
- rubric (page 9) class set of photocopies

Setting the Stage

Review the sound of each letter of the alphabet. Place the letter cards on the floor or on a desk at the front of the room, and have each student choose a letter card. Give each student a magazine and a large sheet of construction paper. Tell students to glue their letter card in the middle of their paper and look through the magazine to find pictures of items that start with their letter. Have them cut out the pictures and glue them to their paper to create a collage. Encourage students to share pictures with others as they find appropriate picture matches. Have them share their completed collages in small groups.

OBJECTIVE

The student will write simple sentences that include alliteration.

CRITICAL COMPONENTS

- Most words in each sentence begin with the same sound.
- Each sentence begins with a capital letter.
- Each sentence ends with the correct punctuation.

Instructional Input

1 Ask students to look at the collage they made in Setting the Stage and create a sentence that includes some of the pictures. Invite volunteers to share their sentence (e.g., *The ant ate the apple. The boy blew bubbles*). Record their responses on the board.

2 Read aloud *Animalia.* Discuss the repetitive use of the letter sounds. Have students write sentences about animals with several words that start with the same sound.

3 Give each student an Animal Word Recognition reproducible. Invite volunteers to identify the animal in each box. Use each animal in several sentences. For example, say *A hippo has short hair on its head. A hippo swims in the water. A hippo lives in Africa.* Tell students to fill in the bubbles next to the words that begin with the same sound as the animal's name. Point out that they will need to fill in more than one bubble for each animal.

4 Display the Animal Word Recognition overhead transparency. Review the correct answers, and have students circle them. After reviewing each answer, ask a volunteer to say a sentence that includes the animal, the words that begin with the same sound, and additional words if necessary. For example, a student might say *An angry ant attacks an alligator* or *Simon the silly squirrel sees strawberries.*

Guided Practice

1 Give each student an Amazing Animals reproducible, and display the overhead transparency. Read aloud the words in the word bank. Then, read aloud each sentence frame. Reread the words in the word bank after each sentence, and tell students to fill in the blanks in each sentence with words that begin with the same sound.

2 Invite volunteers to share their sentences. Review the correct answers for each sentence. Have students think of additional alliterative words for each sentence, and record their responses above the blank lines on the transparency.

3 Invite students to draw a picture of their favorite sentence in the box at the bottom of the page.

Independent Practice

1 Invite students to write three alliterative sentences about an animal. Tell students that they may write their own sentences or use their own words to complete the sentence frames from the Amazing Animals reproducible. (Some students will feel successful creating new, original sentences, while others will feel more confident copying or modifying the cloze activity sentences.)

2 Have students revise and edit their rough draft and then use the rubric to evaluate their writing.

Presentation

- Have students **publish** their final drafts on the Awesome Animals reproducibles and illustrate their sentences on a separate paper.
- Encourage students to **share** their sentences with the whole class or in small groups.
- **Display** student work on a bulletin board titled *Amazing Animals*.

TEACHING HINTS/EXTENSIONS

- Play "Animal Adventure" with the class. Have students sit in a circle. Hold up a flash card of the letter *A*, and say *I went on an animal adventure and I saw an amazing aardvark*. Next, hold up a *B* flash card. Invite the student next to you to say a sentence with an animal and a describing word that start with *B* (e.g., *I went on an animal adventure and I saw a bold baboon*). Continue with the rest of the alphabet. Encourage students to use their imaginations and to help one another. If a student can't think of an animal, brainstorm an invented animal such as a "willowy whinebox."
- Extend alliteration fun to include student names and interests. Begin by printing your name on the board. Invite students to brainstorm describing words that start with the first letter of your name. Record their suggestions on the board. As a class, choose one to three words which best describe you, and write them and your name on a paper headband. Have the class brainstorm alliterative descriptive words for each student's name. Invite students to choose their favorite words, and write them and their name on a headband.

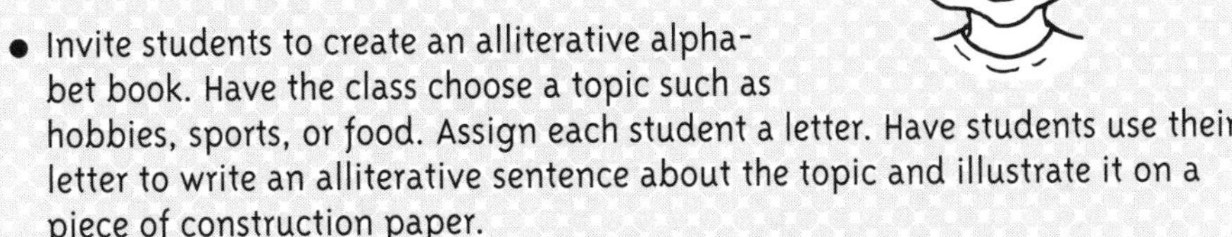

- Invite students to create an alliterative alphabet book. Have the class choose a topic such as hobbies, sports, or food. Assign each student a letter. Have students use their letter to write an alliterative sentence about the topic and illustrate it on a piece of construction paper.
- Have students complete one or more of these writing prompts in a journal:
  - ✔ Use the letter *M* to write an alliterative description of your mom.
  - ✔ Use the letter *D* to write an alliterative description of your dad.
  - ✔ Use the first letter of a friend's name to write an alliterative description of him or her.

Name ____________________ Date ____________________

Animal Word Recognition

Directions: Fill in the bubbles next to the words that start with the same sound as the animal's name. (Hint: There is more than one word for each picture.)

- tiny
- angry
- attacks

- furry
- brings
- big

- silly
- funny
- strawberries

- huge
- large
- hunts

- zany
- striped
- zipper

- cuddles
- cute
- fat

- friendly
- food
- silly

- munches
- large
- mean

Name ______________________ Date ______________________

Amazing Animals

Directions: Complete these sentences so that the words have the same beginning sound. Draw a picture to show your favorite sentence.

1. The big bear brings bananas.

2. The huge hippo hugs hyenas.

3. The cute cat cuddles kittens.

4. The mean mouse munches marbles.

Name ______________________ Date ______________________

Awesome Animals

Directions: Write three sentences about animals. For each sentence, use words that have the same beginning sound.

1. Michelle

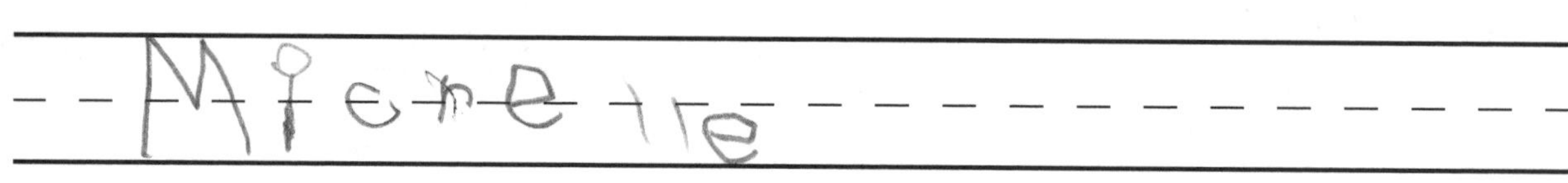

2. LINDA

DAD

3. MOM

Tasty Treats

Preparation

Read aloud books about eating and the sense of taste.

- *Berenstain Bears and Too Much Junk Food* by Stan and Jan Berenstain (Econo-Clad Books)
- *D. W. the Picky Eater* by Marc Brown (Little, Brown and Company)
- *Tasting* by Helen Frost (Capstone Press)

Collect snack items with a variety of tastes (e.g., salty—potato chips and pretzels, spicy—chilies and cheese dip, sweet—jelly beans and chocolate, sour—pickles and lemon drops) for each student. Include at least two items for each taste category.

Prepare a plate of snacks for each student.

Gather white paper for each student.

Make copies of these reproducibles.

- Taste Word Recognition (page 24) transparency, class set of photocopies
- Tasty Treats (page 25) transparency, class set of photocopies
- rubric (page 9) class set of photocopies

Setting the Stage

Write the headings *sour, salty, sweet,* and *spicy* in big letters on the board. Give each student a plate of snacks. Invite students to taste each item one at a time. After the class has enjoyed the snacks, discuss how they taste, and list each item under the appropriate taste category on the board. Encourage students to think of other words that describe the snacks such as *crunchy, delicious, cheesy, creamy,* and *hot.* Record these words next to the foods they describe.

OBJECTIVE

The student will write simple sentences that describe the taste of his or her favorite treats.

CRITICAL COMPONENTS

- Sensory detail words are used to describe the way foods taste.
- Each sentence begins with a capital letter.
- Each sentence ends with the correct punctuation.

Instructional Input

1 Invite students to take turns choosing their favorite snack from the ones they tasted. Ask each student to point to the item and say a sentence that describes its taste. For example, a student might say *My favorite snack is chocolate because it tastes sweet and yummy.*

2 Give each student a Taste Word Recognition reproducible. Invite volunteers to identify the food item in each box. Read aloud each set of words, and then use the words to complete a sentence frame. For example, say *Potato chips taste sweet. Potato chips taste salty. Potato chips taste spicy.* Tell students to fill in the bubble next to the word that best describes how each food item tastes.

3 Display the Taste Word Recognition overhead transparency. Review the correct answers, and have students circle them. For each food item on the reproducible, invite students to say sentences that include the food item, the correct "taste word," and an additional taste word. For example, a student might say *Chili peppers taste spicy and hot.*

Guided Practice

1 Invite students to remember what foods they ate in Setting the Stage. Have them help you spell these words by sounding them out. Record the words on the board.

2 Ask students how each food item tasted. Invite students to sound out these words to help you spell them. Record several responses next to each food.

3 Give each student a Tasty Treats reproducible, and display the overhead transparency. Read aloud the paragraph with the blanks. Reread the paragraph. Tell students to fill in the blanks on their reproducible with the food items they tasted and the words listed below the blanks or words from the board.

4 Review the words students wrote in the blanks. Record their responses on the transparency. If several answers can be correct, record them all on the transparency.

Independent Practice

1 Draw a place mat on a piece of white paper. Tell students what four to six of your favorite treats are. Draw them on the place mat. Leave room for writing below or above each picture. For each treat, write a sentence that describes what it is and how it tastes. For example, you can write *Oranges taste tangy and juicy.*

2 Give each student a piece of white paper. Invite students to sketch a rough draft of their personalized place mat. Remind them to draw their favorite treats and leave room to write sentences that describe the treats. (The number of foods students draw will vary depending on their ability level.) Encourage students to use their reproducible and the list you wrote on the board in Guided Practice as word banks.

3 Have students revise and edit their rough draft and then use the rubric to evaluate their writing.

Presentation

- Have students **publish** their final drafts and draw their favorite treats on construction paper. Show them how to cut off the edges of their paper to create a "place mat." Laminate the completed place mats.
- Encourage students to **share** their place mats in small groups. Ask them to read aloud each sentence as they display their artwork.
- **Display** the place mats at class parties or snacktime parties.

TEACHING HINTS/EXTENSIONS

- Host a "Tasty Treat Party" in your classroom to culminate this activity. Prepare and send home a parent letter to ask for volunteers to help serve food and clean up afterwards. Assign students food items to bring according to their last name. For example, students whose last name begins with A–E could bring fruit or vegetables; F–J could bring snacks (e.g., chips, pretzels); and so on.
- Encourage students to bring a favorite snack item from home in a small brown bag. Have students write on the outside of their bag two to three clues that describe their snack's taste. For example, a student might write *My favorite snack is sweet and juicy. It is crunchy and delicious. I eat one every day for lunch.* (apple) Invite students to bring their bag to the front of the class and share their clues. Have the student who correctly identifies the item share his or her bag.
- Invite students to create their own imaginary food recipes. Have them write their recipes (with assistance, if needed) or draw the ingredients for one or more of the following dishes: Mud Ball Meatloaf, Beastly Brownies, Spider Soup, Dinosaur Delight, or Mixed-Up Martian Mess. Bind together the recipes to create a class book titled *Creative Concoctions*.
- Have students complete one or more of these writing prompts in a journal:
  - ✔ Describe the tastes of the foods you eat for breakfast.
  - ✔ Write about what you like to eat for lunch and what each food tastes like.
  - ✔ Describe your favorite dinner and what each food tastes like.

10/28/06

Name Michelle Date

Taste Word Recognition

Directions: Fill in the bubble next to the word that best describes how the food item tastes.

- sweet
- spicy
- salty

- salty
- sweet
- spicy

- salty
- spicy
- sour

- salty
- sour
- sweet

- sweet
- spicy
- salty

- sweet
- spicy
- sour

- salty
- sweet
- spicy

- sweet
- salty
- sour

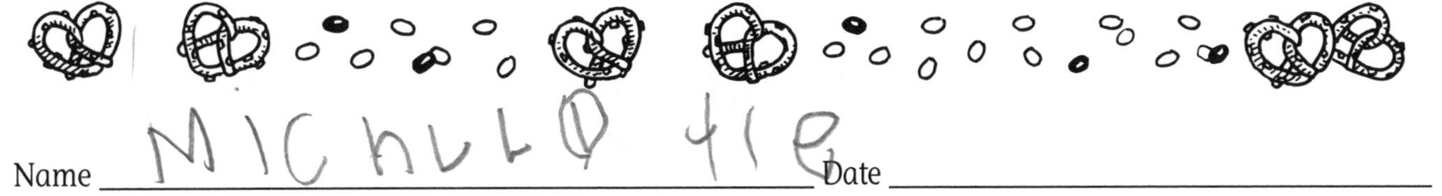

Name MICHLLE HIE Date ______________________

Tasty Treats

Directions: Fill in the blanks with foods you ate and with one of the words in the parentheses that describe how they tasted.

I ate many treats during this lesson. I enjoyed eating

______________________ that were ______________________.
(sour, salty, sweet, spicy)

I also ate some crunchy ______________________ that were

______________________. My taste buds woke up when I ate
(sour, salty, sweet, spicy)

some hot ______________________ that were

______________________. My mouth puckered when I ate some
(sour, salty, sweet, spicy)

______________________ that were ______________________.
(sour, salty, sweet, spicy)

I Spy

Preparation

Read aloud books about zoo animals.

- *Bembo's Zoo: An Animal ABC Book* by Roberto de Vicq de Cumptich (The Millbrook Press)
- *Bobby's Zoo* by Carolyn Lunn (Children's Press)
- *Dear Zoo* by Rod Campbell (Simon & Schuster)

Gather three to five pieces of chart paper.

Collect color pictures and posters of zoo animals.

Make copies of these reproducibles.

- Sight Word Recognition (page 29) transparency, class set of photocopies
- City Zoo (page 30) transparency, class set of photocopies
- Animal Pinwheel (page 31) teacher photocopy and class set of photocopies on card stock
- rubric (page 9) class set of photocopies

Prepare a sample animal pinwheel. (See Independent Practice.)

OBJECTIVE

The student will write simple descriptions of zoo animals.

CRITICAL COMPONENTS

- Four zoo animals are described.
- Sensory detail words are used to describe what each animal looks like.
- Each description includes appropriate vocabulary.

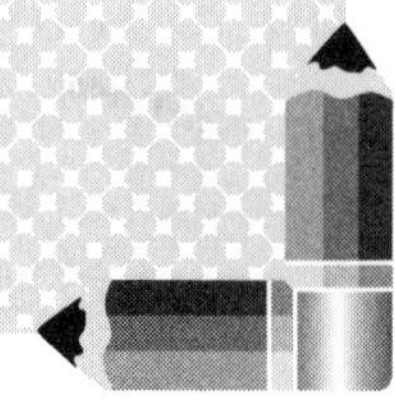

Setting the Stage

Show students the color pictures and posters of zoo animals. Ask students to sound out the names of the zoo animals in the pictures as you write them on a piece of chart paper. Encourage students to brainstorm names of other zoo animals, and record their responses on the chart paper. Discuss each animal and what students know about it.

Instructional Input

1 Select a picture of your favorite zoo animal. Write the name of the animal on another piece of chart paper, and ask students to list as many of its physical characteristics as possible. Record their responses on the chart paper. For example, for a giraffe students might say *long neck, long front legs, spotted skin pattern, pointed ears, long tongue, short mane, short knobby horns,* and *tan and brown coloring.*

2 Invite students to sit in a circle. Ask a volunteer to pick an animal picture. Write the animal's name on another piece of chart paper. Have the volunteer describe one aspect of the animal's appearance in one or two words or a complete sentence. Record the response under the animal's name on the chart paper. Ask the volunteer to pass the picture to the student sitting to his or her left, and encourage this student to describe another aspect of the animal's appearance. Record his or her response. Continue this process until students cannot think of any more descriptions. Invite the last student who gave a description to choose a new animal picture, and have the class repeat the process. Record each animal's characteristics on a separate piece of chart paper. Continue this activity until the class has created descriptive lists for several animals.

Polar Bear
four legs
pointy nose
white fur
black nose
big feet
round ears

Elephant
big ears
wrinkled skin
gray coloring
long trunk
long white tusks
skinny tail

Guided Practice

1 Give each student a Sight Word Recognition reproducible. Invite volunteers to identify the animal in each box. Read aloud each set of words, and then use the words to complete a sentence frame. For example, say *An elephant has long arms. An elephant has a trunk. An elephant has spots.* Tell students to fill in the bubble next to the word that best describes a physical characteristic of each animal.

2 Display the Sight Word Recognition overhead transparency. Review the correct answers, and have students circle them. For each animal, invite students to say sentences that include the animal's name, the correct descriptive word, and another word or phrase that describes the animal's physical appearance. For example, a student might say *A kangaroo has a pouch and a long thick tail.*

3 Give each student a City Zoo reproducible, and display the overhead transparency. Read aloud the paragraph with the blanks. Reread the paragraph, and tell students to fill in the blanks with words from the word banks.

4 Review the words that students wrote in the blanks. Record their responses on the transparency. Tell students to write the correct answers if they wrote an incorrect word.

Independent Practice

1 Give each student a piece of lined paper, and invite students to fold it in fourths (in half horizontally and then in half vertically).

2 Have students write the name of a zoo animal and two or three descriptive words or phrases about it in each section. For example, a student might write *Lion: bushy mane, gold fur,* and *long tail.* Encourage students to use the descriptive word lists you recorded on chart paper in Instructional Input as word banks.

3 Have students revise and edit their rough draft and then evaluate their writing.

4 Use your sample animal pinwheel to demonstrate how to make a pinwheel. Use the following directions as a guide. Cut out the square, and cut along the dark inside lines to the points. Fold the numbered corners to the center point, and attach them with a brass fastener. Write the names of four animals on the folded flaps, and write descriptions on the lines. Make a small hole in the top of a straw with a pin or scissors. Attach the brass fastener to the straw.

Presentation

- Have students **create** pinwheels using the Animal Pinwheel reproducible, a brass fastener, and a straw.
- Have students **write** final drafts of their zoo animals' names and the descriptive words or phrases about them on the pinwheels.
- Encourage students to **share** their pinwheels with the class. Compare and contrast student descriptions of the same animal.
- **Display** the pinwheels in buckets or pots filled with a small amount of sand.

TEACHING HINTS/EXTENSIONS

- Help students create interesting descriptive sentences during a game of "I Went to the Zoo." Ask one student to put on a cap or hat to represent the zookeeper and complete this sentence frame: *I went to the zoo and I saw a(n)* __________ *with* __________. For example, a student might say *I went to the zoo and I saw an elephant with a long gray trunk*. Have the next student repeat the first sentence and then add a second animal and visual description. If students are having trouble stringing together the sentences, write each sentence on the board or on sentence strips, or forget the repetition and have students complete the sentence frame with their animal and description.
- Trace and cut out simple animal shapes from butcher paper or tagboard. Have students use tempera paint to add "skin" or "fur" to the animal cutouts. Invite them to use some of the following variations to add texture and interest to their animals: liquid starch will make a sleek "coat"; soap flakes mixed with paint will create furry-looking animals; sawdust, sand, or rinsed coffee grounds will make a rough coat.
- Visit a zoo on a class field trip. Invite students to bring cameras and take photographs of the animals. Have them draw pictures of animals, and display the drawings next to the photographs.
- Have students complete one or more of these writing prompts in a journal:
  - ✔ Imagine yourself flying through space. Describe what you see.
  - ✔ Imagine yourself swimming underwater in the ocean. Describe what you see.
  - ✔ Imagine yourself on a trip to a faraway land. Where would you go? Describe what you see.

Name ______________________________ Date ____________________

Sight Word Recognition

Directions: Fill in the bubble next to the description that best matches the animal's physical appearance.

○ long arms
● trunk
○ spots

● long arms
○ mane
○ hump

○ trunk
○ long arms
● long neck

○ trunk
○ spots
● pouch

○ pouch
● mane
○ stripes

● spots
○ hump
○ long neck

○ spots
● stripes
○ pouch

● hump
○ long arms
○ stripes

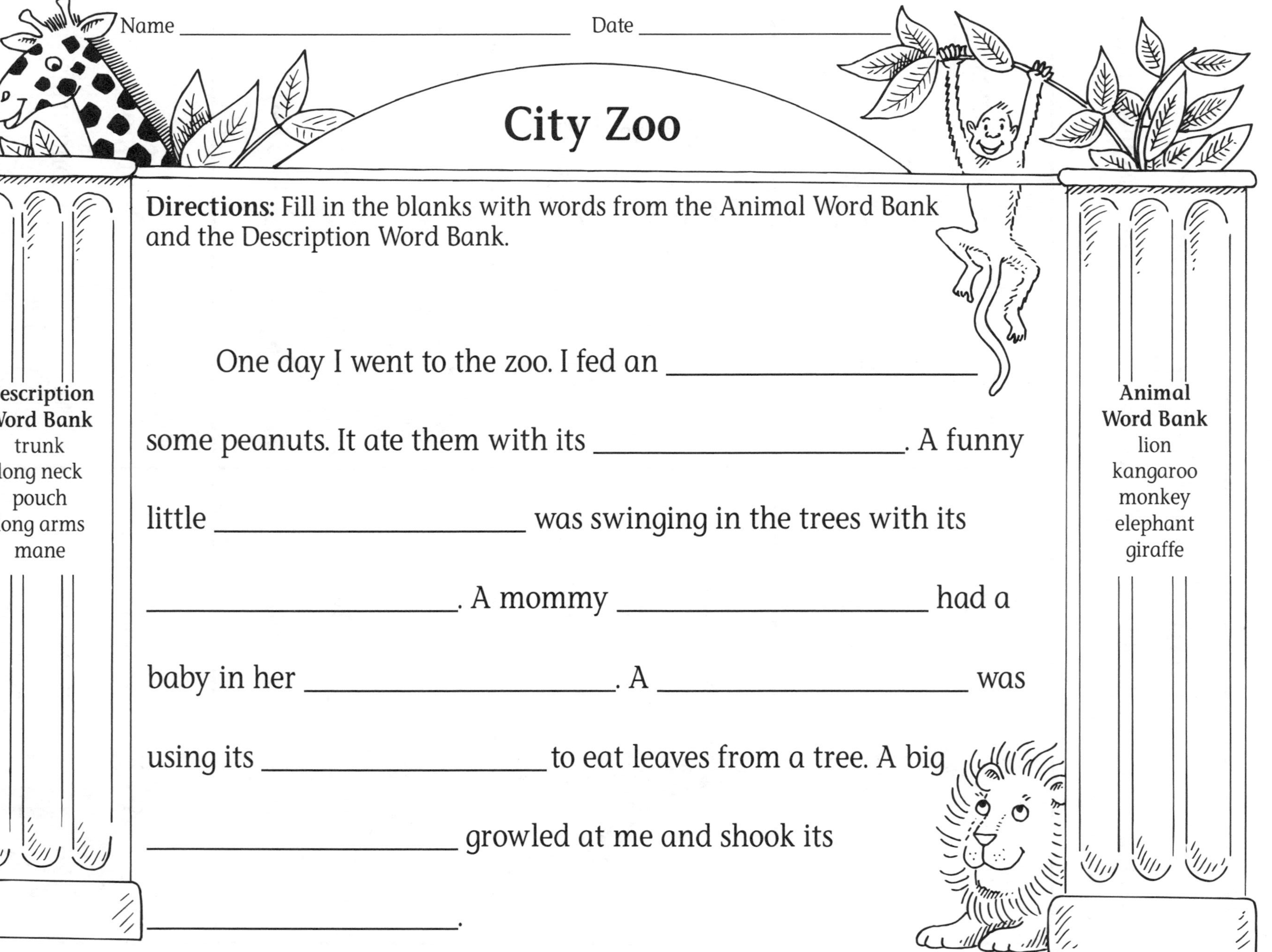

Name ____________________ Date ____________

City Zoo

Directions: Fill in the blanks with words from the Animal Word Bank and the Description Word Bank.

Description Word Bank
trunk
long neck
pouch
long arms
mane

Animal Word Bank
lion
kangaroo
monkey
elephant
giraffe

One day I went to the zoo. I fed an ____________ some peanuts. It ate them with its ____________. A funny little ____________ was swinging in the trees with its ____________. A mommy ____________ had a baby in her ____________. A ____________ was using its ____________ to eat leaves from a tree. A big ____________ growled at me and shook its ____________.

Animal Pinwheel

Directions

1. Cut out the square.
2. Cut along the dark inside lines to the end points.
3. Fold the numbered corners to the center point. Attach them with a brass fastener.
4. Write the name of a zoo animal on each folded flap.
5. Write two or three descriptions of each animal on the writing lines.
6. Attach the brass fastener to a straw.

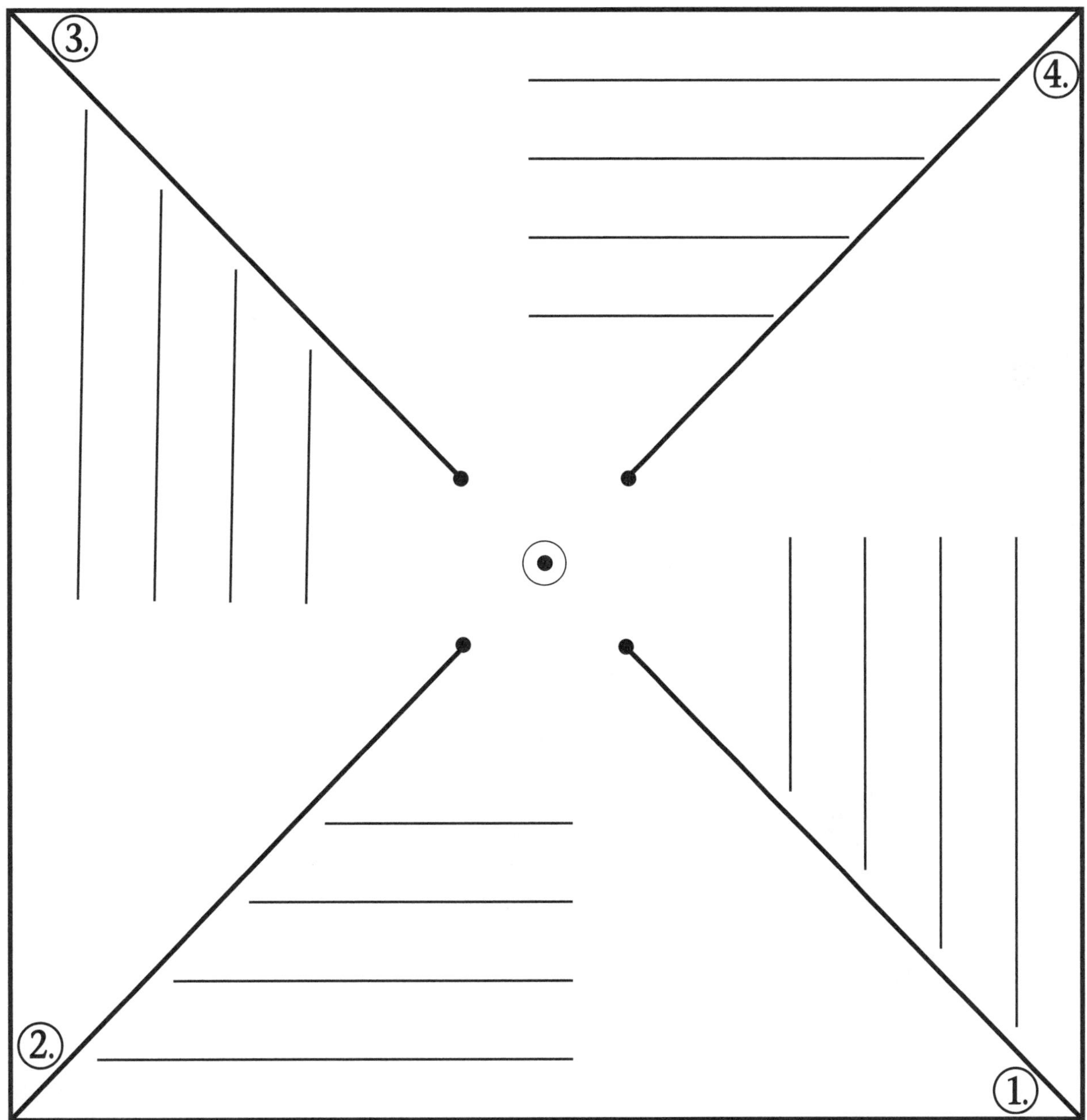

Rhyme Time

Preparation

Read aloud books that include rhyming words and poems.

- *Giraffe and a Half* by Shel Silverstein (HarperCollins)
- *I Can Read With My Eyes Shut!* by Dr. Seuss (Random House)
- *The New Kid on the Block* by Jack Prelutsky (Greenwillow Books)

Gather construction paper for each student and chart paper.

Make copies of these reproducibles.

- Draw a Beast (page 35) transparency
- Rhyme Word Recognition (page 36) transparency, class set of photocopies
- Did You Ever See? (page 37) transparency, class set of photocopies
- rubric (page 9) class set of photocopies

OBJECTIVE

The student will write simple rhyming sentences (couplets).

CRITICAL COMPONENTS

- Each couplet has two lines.
- The last word in each line shares the same sound pattern.
- Each sentence begins with a capital letter.
- Each sentence ends with the correct punctuation.

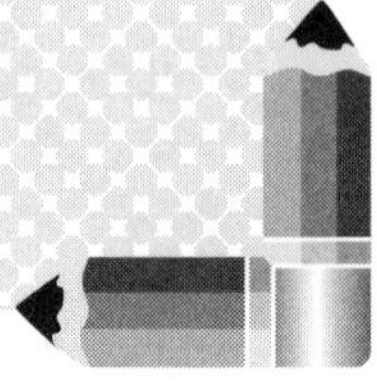

Setting the Stage

Read aloud several poems. Ask students what rhyming words are. Explain that rhyming words sound the same and that although some letters are different, they share a common sound (usually the vowel and ending sound). Reread the poems, and encourage students to identify the rhyming words. Record these words on chart paper. Have the class play "What Doesn't Belong?" Recite a list of four words: three words that rhyme and one that does not (e.g., *bat, cat, top, hat*). Have students listen to determine which word does not belong. Repeat the words, and encourage students to stand, clap, pat their heads, or give some other predetermined signal when they hear the word that does not rhyme. Repeat the game several times with new sets of words. Then, invite students to become the leader and say word lists.

Instructional Input

1 Review the rhyming words you recorded in Setting the Stage. Read aloud the words that rhyme, and invite students to tell you more words that rhyme with them. Add new words to the list.

2 Display the Draw a Beast overhead transparency. Read aloud the poem with the blanks. Reread the poem. For each line, invite students to say a word that rhymes with the last word in the previous sentence to fill in the blank. If students give several responses, ask the class to vote on one word to record on the transparency. Read aloud the completed poem.

3 Give each student a piece of construction paper. Read aloud the completed poem, and invite students to draw a beast by following the directions in the poem. After students have completed their beast, invite a volunteer to read the poem aloud. Create your own beast on the board as he or she reads the directions. Encourage students to share their beast with the class.

Guided Practice

1 Give each student a Rhyme Word Recognition reproducible. Invite volunteers to identify the object in each box. Read aloud each set of words. Tell students to fill in the bubble next to the word that rhymes with the object.

2 Display the Rhyme Word Recognition overhead transparency. Review the correct answers, and have students circle them.

3 Give each student a Did You Ever See? reproducible, and display the overhead transparency. Read aloud the words in the word bank, and then read aloud each couplet. Have students write the correct rhyming word in each couplet. Review the answers, and then record them on the transparency. Encourage students to write the correct answer if they wrote an incorrect word.

Independent Practice

1 Write on the board or on a sentence strip *Did you ever see a __________?*

2 Invite students to write three of their own rhyming couplets. Encourage them to use the lists of rhyming words you recorded on chart paper in Setting the Stage and Instructional Input and their completed reproducible as word banks. Have them pick pairs of words and then write sentences that include the two words. Encourage struggling students to copy or modify their favorite sentences from the Did You Ever See? reproducible.

3 Have students revise and edit their rough draft and then use the rubric to evaluate their writing.

Presentation

- Have students **publish** their final drafts on white paper or construction paper and illustrate their favorite sentence at the bottom of the page.
- Encourage students to **present** their couplets and illustration to the class. Invite students to leave off the last word in each couplet, and have the class identify the rhyming word.
- **Create** a class book titled *Room ___'s Rhyme Time.*

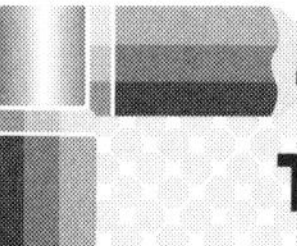

TEACHING HINTS/EXTENSIONS

- Host a "poetry picnic" on a grassy area at your school. Invite parents or another class to attend, and have them sit on blankets or sheets on the ground. Print a program to hand out. Have students read their couplets and show their illustrations.
- Cut a large shape from a piece of butcher paper. Tape the front side of small envelopes to the paper. Label the back of each envelope with a different ending phonogram (e.g., *-at, -ike, -ant, -or, -ank, -ark, -eet, -old, -ive, -ice, -ain, -ock, -ack*). Place blank sheets of paper in each envelope, and invite students to write rhyming words for each ending sound on the paper. For example, students might write *cold, gold, sold, told, mold,* and *hold* for *-old*. Encourage students to visit the "poetry pockets" to get ideas for rhyming words to use in their writing.

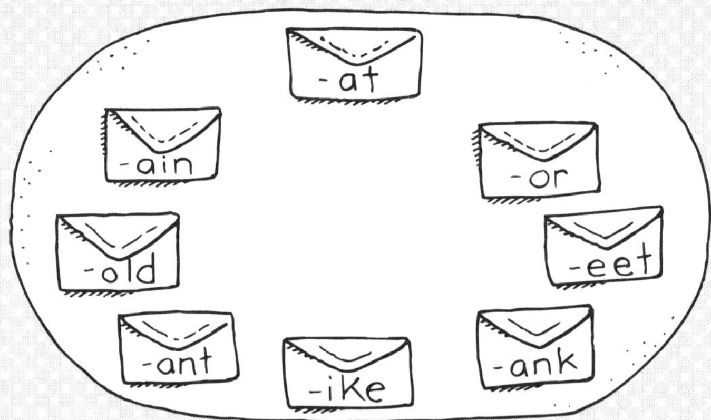

- Play this game with your students during P. E. or recess. Write simple ending phonograms (e.g., *-old, -ock, -ant*) on index cards. Have a student choose a card, read aloud the phonogram, and say a rhyming word. As soon as the student says the rhyming word, have the other students begin running. Invite the "reader" to tag another student who will then think of a new rhyming word. Play until a student cannot think of another rhyming word. Continue the game by asking the student to choose a new card.
- Have students complete one or more of these writing prompts in a journal:
  - ✔ Create a rhyme about a pet.
  - ✔ Create a rhyme about food.
  - ✔ Create a rhyme about a friend or relative.

Draw a Beast

Directions: Fill in each blank with a word that rhymes with the last word in the previous sentence.

To draw a beast, get out of bed.
Grab a crayon and draw a ______________________.

His face looks like a great big pie.
Quickly add a giant ______________________.

He needs something to talk and eat.
Give him a mouth that looks so ______________________.

To give him something that he blows,
Our beast will need a great big ______________________.

To make his head less round and bare,
Give our friend some curly ______________________.

His face is done. Let's double-check.
I think that we should add a ______________________.

His body must be oh so strong.
Make it fat and very ______________________.

We must add legs so he can run.
Give him three to add some ______________________.

Add some arms. Oh what a treat.
I'm pretty sure he needs some ______________________.

On his arms, he wears rubber bands.
To keep them on, he needs two ______________________.

Our beast is done. Now you can rest.
I'm sure that he's the very ______________________.

Name ______________________________ Date ______________________

Rhyme Word Recognition

Directions: Fill in the bubble next to the word that rhymes with the object.

○ hat
○ well
○ note

○ hive
○ snap
○ cake

○ coat
○ fly
○ jam

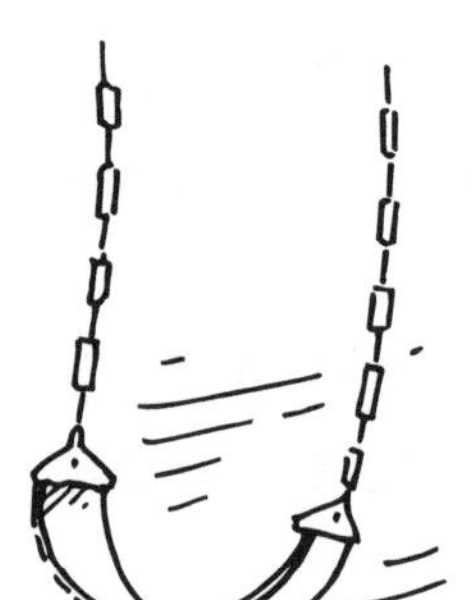

○ bell
○ bring
○ lake

○ top
○ bride
○ saw

○ rat
○ far
○ cone

○ swing
○ jar
○ cat

○ date
○ bat
○ wing

Name ______________________________ Date ____________________

Did You Ever See?

Directions: Complete each sentence by writing a rhyming word in the blank.

Did you ever see a rat
with a baseball ______________________?

Did you ever see a whale
with a red-striped ______________________?

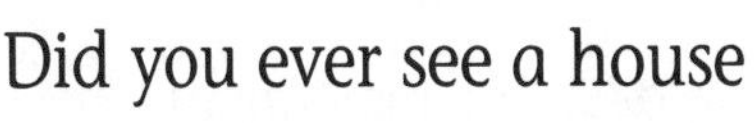

Did you ever see a house
owned by a ______________________?

Did you ever see a pig
dance a little ______________________?

Did you ever see a snake
eat a piece of birthday ______________________?

Did you ever see a snail
with a hammer and ______________________?

Did you ever see a dog
asleep on a ______________________?

Did you ever see a fly
wear a polka-dot ______________________?

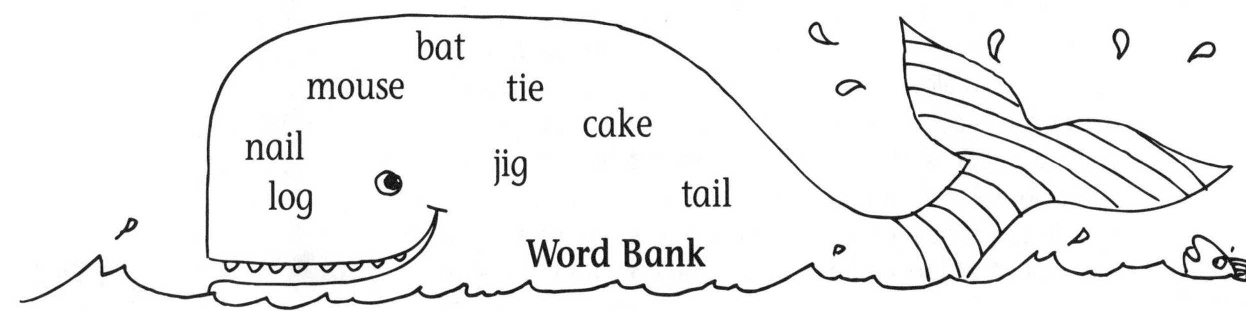

Animal Antics

Preparation

Read aloud books about animals' movements.

- *Commotion in the Ocean* by Giles Andreae (Tiger Tales)
- *Elephants Swim* by Linda Capus Riley (Houghton Mifflin)
- *Wiggle Waggle* by Jonathan London (Silver Whistle)

Label large index cards with the words *run, walk, crawl, hop, fly,* and *climb.*

Gather chart paper and yarn.

Make copies of these reproducibles.

- Verb Word Recognition (page 41) transparency, class set of photocopies
- ____'s Amazing Antics (page 42) teacher photocopy and one photocopy for every four students on card stock
- Chain Movement Strips (page 43) teacher photocopy and class set of photocopies on card stock
- My Busy Day (page 44) transparency, class set of photocopies
- rubric (page 9) class set of photocopies

Prepare a sample movement chain. (See Guided Practice.)

OBJECTIVE

The student will write simple sentences that describe movement.

CRITICAL COMPONENTS

- Verbs are used to describe animals' movements.
- Each sentence begins with a capital letter.
- Each sentence ends with the correct punctuation.

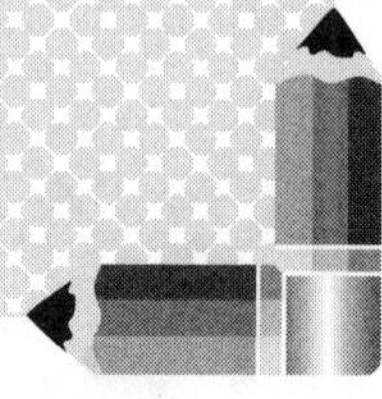

Setting the Stage

Have the class play relay games that will introduce students to movement verbs. Divide the class into three or four teams, and designate an area to start and end the race. Show students the word cards, read them aloud, and demonstrate how students will perform each action by comparing it to an animal's movement. For example, tell students to walk bent over with the tips of their hands touching the ground like an elephant walks. To begin the relay, show one card, and say the word aloud. Have every student on each team perform this action during the relay. Continue the game until you have read all the cards. Vary the relay by interspersing the movements. For example, call out a new verb in the middle of a relay, and tell all students to then switch to that form of movement and continue the relay.

Instructional Input

1 Ask students to name animals and use verbs to describe the way they move. Record the animals and the movements they make on chart paper. Encourage students to pantomime these movements and create sentences that describe them. For example, a student might say *Snakes slither in the grass.*

2 Ask students *Can you swim, climb, hop, slither, or fly?* Invite students to name the movements (verbs) in the question, and record their responses on the board. Encourage students to generate sentences about themselves performing these movements. For example, a student might say *I climb big trees in my grandma's backyard.*

3 Give each student a Verb Word Recognition reproducible. Invite volunteers to identify the animal in each box. Read aloud each set of words, and then use the words to complete a sentence frame. For example, say *Monkeys fly. Monkeys climb. Monkeys swim.* Tell students to fill in the bubble next to the word that best describes how the animal moves.

4 Display the Verb Word Recognition overhead transparency. Review the correct answers, and have students circle them.

Guided Practice

1 Give each student one square from the ____'s Amazing Antics reproducible, and have students fill in their name and draw a picture of themselves.

2 Give each student a Chain Movement Strips reproducible. Read aloud the sentence starters. Tell students to complete each sentence with a different movement. Encourage them to use the word list you recorded in Instructional Input as a word bank. Help students add interesting details to their sentences. For example, a student might write *My favorite way to move is to swim in the ocean.*

3 Show students the sample movement chain you prepared. Have students cut apart their strips, link the chains, and connect the ends with glue or tape. Ask them to hole-punch their Amazing Antics card and attach it to the chain with a piece of yarn.

Independent Practice

1 Display the My Busy Day overhead transparency. Ask students to help you write about your day by describing your movements. For example, you might write *Today, I ran after my dog Aussie. I walked to my car in the driveway. I drove to work on the highway.* Tell students that they should say sentences in chronological order so they "flow" like a story.

2 Invite students to write sentences about the ways they move when they are in their classroom and when they play outside at school. Encourage students to use the word list you recorded in Instructional Input as a word bank.

3 Have students revise and edit their rough draft and then use the rubric to evaluate their writing.

Presentation

- Have students **publish** their final drafts on the My Busy Day reproducibles.
- Encourage students to **share** their final draft with the class.
- **Create** a class book titled *We Are Busy Students.*
- **Display** the movement chains by hanging them from the ceiling or light fixtures around the classroom.

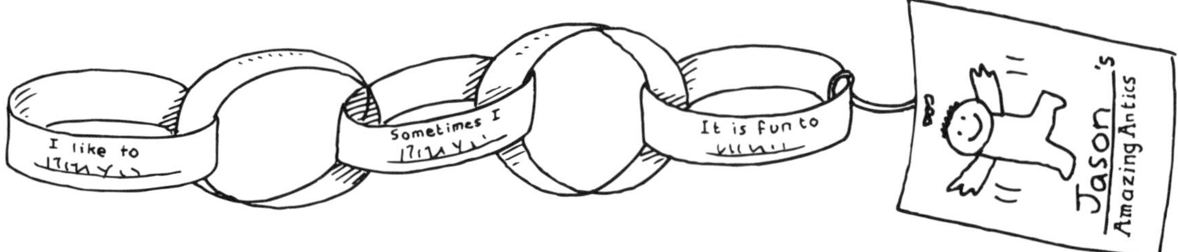

TEACHING HINTS/EXTENSIONS

- Invite a school staff member such as a custodian, cook, crossing guard, or secretary to visit your classroom and share the actions and movements that are part of his or her job. Have students write about the movements this person performs as part of his or her job.
- Have students bring in a photo of themselves enjoying a movement activity such as playing ball, swinging, or swimming. Ask them to show their picture and tell about the experience. Invite students to write about their picture, and post the photos and descriptions on a bulletin board titled *Room __ in Motion.*
- Give students magazines. (*National Geographic* is wonderful for this activity.) Encourage them to choose a movement such as running or swimming and create a collage of people and animals demonstrating this action.
- Have students complete one or more of these writing prompts in a journal:
  - ✔ Use interesting verbs to describe how you play on a playground.
  - ✔ Use interesting verbs to describe how to play a sport.
  - ✔ Use several verbs to describe how to get ready for school.

Name ______________________________ Date ______________________

Verb Word Recognition

Directions: Fill in the bubble next to the word that best describes how the animal moves.

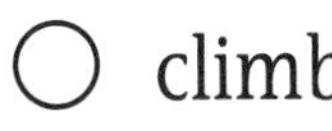

- ○ fly
- ○ climb
- ○ swim

- ○ run
- ○ fly
- ○ hop

- ○ slither
- ○ fly
- ○ run

- ○ walk
- ○ swim
- ○ hop

- ○ swim
- ○ run
- ○ walk

- ○ crawl
- ○ run
- ○ hop

- ○ swim
- ○ fly
- ○ hop

- ○ run
- ○ play
- ○ crawl

______________________'s Amazing Antics	______________________'s Amazing Antics
______________________'s Amazing Antics	______________________'s Amazing Antics

Chain Movement Strips

I like to

_______________________________.

I also like to

_______________________________.

Sometimes I

_______________________________.

It is fun to

_______________________________.

My favorite way to move is to

_______________________________.

My Busy Day

By

What's My Sound?

Preparation

Read aloud books about farm animals and the sounds they make.

- *Big Red Barn* by Margaret Wise Brown (HarperCollins)
- *The Day the Dog Said, "Cock a Doodle Doo!"* by David McPhail (Scholastic)
- *Mr. Brown Can Moo! Can You?* by Dr. Seuss (Random House)

Collect small plastic farm animals, or place farm animal stickers on index cards. Place an animal or an index card in a brown lunch bag for each student. (You need two of each animal.)

Gather chart paper.

Make copies of these reproducibles.

- Farm Sounds Word Recognition (page 48) transparency, class set of photocopies
- Farm Fun (page 49) transparency, class set of photocopies
- Barn Book (page 50) class set of photocopies
- rubric (page 9) class set of photocopies

OBJECTIVE

The student will write a story that includes simple sentences that describe sounds made by farm animals.

CRITICAL COMPONENTS

- Sensory detail words are used to describe farm animal sounds.
- Each sentence begins with a capital letter.
- Each sentence ends with the correct punctuation.

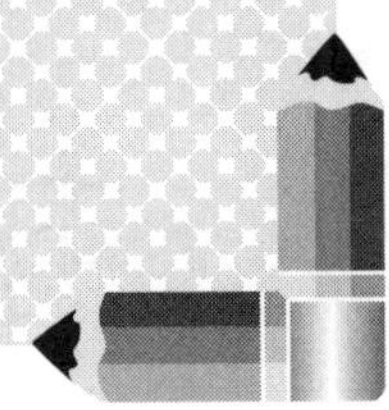

Setting the Stage

Ask students if they have ever visited a farm. Invite them to share their experiences. Ask students what kinds of animals were on the farms they visited or on the farms described in the books you read aloud during the preceding week. Record their responses on a piece of chart paper. Have the class play the "Noisy Animal Game." Show students some of the animals in the brown bags, and have them imitate the sounds the animals make. Give each student a bag. Invite students to quickly peek into their bag and then close it. Tell students that they will be looking for another student who has the same animal and that they will find their match by walking around the room, imitating their animal's sound, and listening to find the other student who is making the same sound. Tell students to sit down next to their "animal match" when they find each other. (Depending on the size of your class, you may want to do this activity with half the class at a time.)

Instructional Input

1 Review the list of farm animals you recorded on chart paper in Setting the Stage, and add other farm animals that students name. As you read aloud each animal's name, ask students to imitate the sound the animal makes. Record the appropriate sound next to each animal's name.

2 Give each student a Farm Sounds Word Recognition reproducible. Invite volunteers to identify the animal in each box. Read aloud each set of words, and then use the words to complete a sentence frame. For example, say *A rooster says gobble-gobble. A rooster says baa. A rooster says cock-a-doodle-doo.* Tell students to fill in the bubble next to the sound the animal makes.

3 Display the Farm Sounds Word Recognition overhead transparency. Review the correct answers, and have students circle them. Encourage students to say their own sentences that include each animal and the sound it makes. For example, a student might say *The little chicks say peep as they waddle around the yard.*

Guided Practice

1 Give each student a Farm Fun reproducible, and display the overhead transparency. Read aloud the paragraph with the blanks. Reread the paragraph, and tell students to fill in the blanks with names of animals from the picture and the sounds they make.

2 Review the words that students wrote in the blanks. Record their responses on the transparency. Tell students to write the correct answer if they wrote an incorrect word.

3 Invite students to write the sound each animal makes beside its picture. Encourage students to refer to the list of animals and their sounds you recorded in Instructional Input.

Independent Practice

1 Invite students to imagine they are farm animals. Ask each student to tell you what farm animal he or she would like to be.

2 Invite students to write a story about their day living on a farm as that animal. Remind them to include animal sounds in the story.

3 Have students revise and edit their rough draft and then use the rubric to evaluate their writing.

Presentation

- Have students **publish** their final drafts on the Barn Book reproducibles and draw pictures above their writing. (If students need more writing lines, photocopy additional pages, or have students trace the barn shape on lined paper.)
- Have students **create** front and back covers for their shape book by cutting out the barn shape, tracing it on construction paper, and cutting out their tracings. Then, have them staple all their pages together to make individual books.
- Encourage students to **share** their barn books with a partner or small group.
- **Display** the books at a learning center or in your classroom library.

TEACHING HINTS/EXTENSIONS

- Read aloud *Brown Bear, Brown Bear, What Do You See?* by Bill Martin Jr. (Henry Holt and Company). Have students use the structure in the book to create a stanza for a poem titled "Farm Animals, Farm Animals, What Do You Hear?"

> Spotted cow, spotted cow,
> What do you hear?
> I hear a feathered turkey
> Gobbling at me!
>
> Feathered turkey, feathered turkey,
> What do you hear?
> I hear a muddy pig
> Oinking at me!

- Use animal stickers to create number cards for 1–9. For example, use one cow sticker for number 1, two horse stickers for number 2, and so on. Include one blank card for zero. Place the cards at a learning center. Have students place the cards facedown in a pile. Invite them to draw two cards at a time and record on a piece of paper an addition or subtraction problem that includes the two numbers. Ask students to solve the problems.
- Invite students to use the tune "Here We Go Around the Mulberry Bush" to create a song about farm animals' sounds. For example:
  The lambs on the farm say, baa, baa, baa, baa, baa, baa, baa, baa, baa.
  The lambs on the farm say, baa, baa, baa, so early in the morning.
  The pigs on the farm say, oink, oink, oink, oink, oink, oink, oink, oink, oink.
  The pigs on the farm say, oink, oink, oink, so early in the morning.
- Have students complete one or more of these writing prompts in a journal:
  - ✔ Imagine you are in your family's car and there are lots of other cars around you. Write about what you hear.
  - ✔ Write about what you hear when you play on the playground.
  - ✔ Imagine you are under the ocean. Write about what you hear.

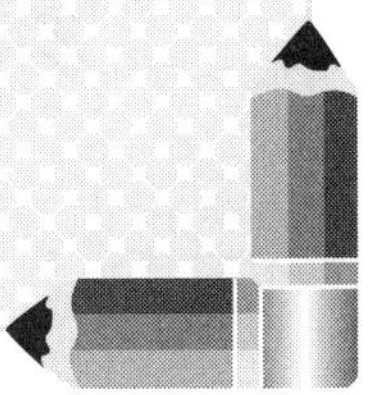

Name ______________________________ Date ______________________

Farm Sounds Word Recognition

Directions: Fill in the bubble next to the sound the animal makes.

○ gobble-gobble

○ baa

○ cock-a-doodle-doo

○ baa

○ honk

○ moo

○ peep

○ honk

○ moo

○ peep

○ honk

○ gobble-gobble

○ moo

○ oink

○ neigh

○ baa

○ neigh

○ honk

○ peep

● gobble-gobble

○ moo

○ cock-a-doodle-doo

○ baa

○ oink

Name ______________________________ Date ______________________________

Farm Fun

Directions: Fill in the blanks with names of the animals from the picture below and the sounds they make.

I woke up early in the morning when I heard the ____________________ crowing ____________________. I looked out the window and saw the farmer's wife throwing corn to the ____________________ who thanked her by saying ____________________. The ____________________ was milking the ____________________ who said ____________________. I went out to the barnyard and saw the white fluffy ____________________who said good morning by bleating ____________________ . On my way back to the house, I saw the fat, pink ____________________. It squealed ____________________ at me.

rooster

horse

chicks

lamb

cow

farmer

pig

Barn Book

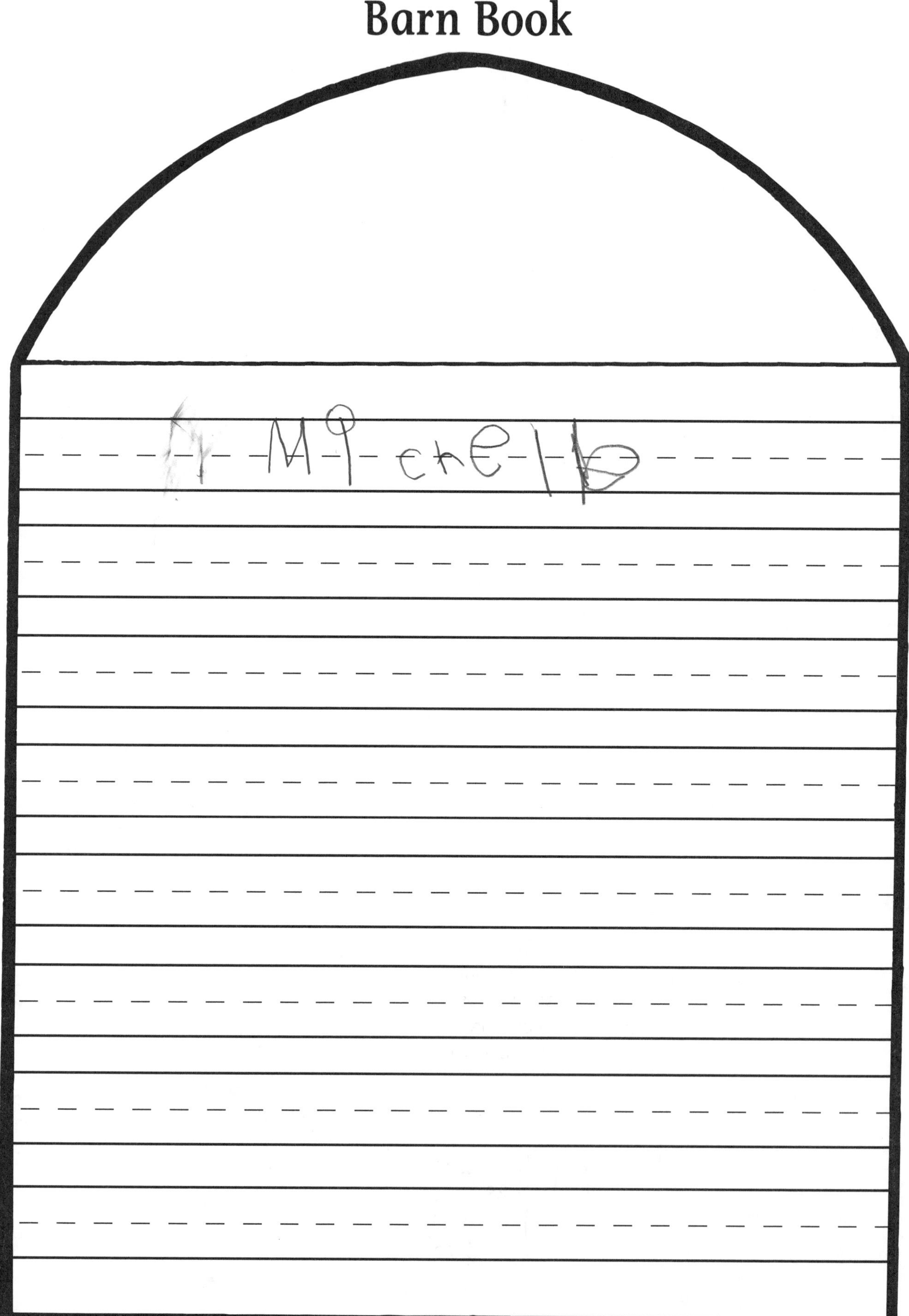

Bunny Tales

Preparation

Read aloud books about bunnies.

- *Bunny Party* by Rosemary Wells (Penguin Putnam)
- *Grumpy Bunnies* by Willy Welch (Charlesbridge Publishing)
- *What Have You Done, Davy?* by Brigitte Weninger (North-South Books)

Collect a bunny puppet or stuffed animal or pictures of bunnies.

Display a clothesline with clothespins attached to it along a wall at a height students can reach.

Gather three pieces of chart paper.

Make copies of these reproducibles.

- Bunny Shirt (page 54) class set of photocopies on different colors of construction paper
- Bunny Word Recognition (page 55) transparency, class set of photocopies
- writing template (page 56) class set of photocopies
- rubric (page 9) class set of photocopies

OBJECTIVE

The student will write one to three sentences that describe a bunny.

CRITICAL COMPONENTS

- Each sentence and each proper noun begin with a capital letter.
- Each sentence ends with the correct punctuation.
- Sentences include adjectives that describe the bunny's habits, looks, or personality.

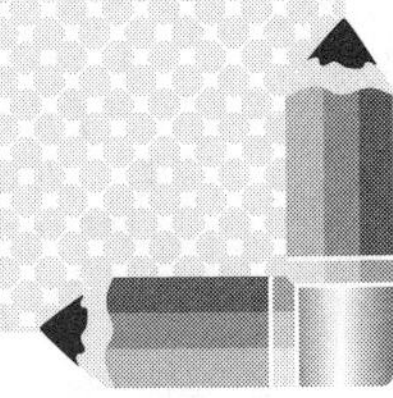

Setting the Stage

Ask a volunteer to stand at the front of the classroom. Ask the class to describe this person. Record describing words (adjectives) on the board. Explain that students have just listed adjectives—words that describe a noun (a person, place, or thing). Invite the class to brainstorm a list of adjectives that describe how someone or something looks, and record their responses on a piece of chart paper. Then, invite the class to brainstorm a list of adjectives that describe how a person or an animal acts or behaves, and record their responses on another piece of chart paper. Write any antonyms next to each other (e.g., big–small, fast–slow). Encourage students to add adjectives to the lists as they think of them or come across them in their daily reading.

Instructional Input

1 Show students the bunny puppet or stuffed animal or pictures of bunnies. Invite them to brainstorm nouns and adjectives that describe a bunny. Record on a third piece of chart paper a list of bunny body parts and adjectives that describe them (e.g., skinny whiskers, long ears, fat body) and a list that describes how a bunny acts or behaves (e.g., fast, silly, nice).

2 Give each student a Bunny Shirt reproducible. Invite students to write an adjective that describes a bunny in big letters and draw an illustration of the word on the remaining area of the shirt.

3 Invite students to cut out their bunny shirt. Ask each student to show his or her shirt to the class, use the adjective in a sentence that describes the bunny, and clip the shirt on the clothesline.

Guided Practice

1 Give each student a Bunny Word Recognition reproducible. Invite volunteers to identify the picture in each box. Say several sentences about the bunny body part. For example, say *A bunny has a pink nose. Its nose is small. I like to see a bunny wiggle its nose.* Tell students to fill in the bubble next to the word that best describes the picture.

2 Display the Bunny Word Recognition overhead transparency. Review the correct answers, and have students circle them.

3 Display the lists of adjectives you recorded in Setting the Stage and Instructional Input, and invite students to read aloud the words as you point to them for review.

4 Have students say sentences that describe how bunnies look and act. Encourage them to use many adjectives in their descriptions. Record their sentences on the board or a piece of chart paper.

Independent Practice

1 Write on the board *What is the bunny's name? What does the bunny look like? What is it wearing? What kind of personality does it have? What is it doing?* Read aloud the questions.

2 Invite students to sketch a bunny and write one to three sentences that describe it. Tell them to use the questions on the board as a guide. Remind them to capitalize the name of the bunny (proper noun). Encourage students to write a complete story if they wish.

3 Have students revise and edit their rough draft and then use the rubric to evaluate their writing.

Presentation

- Have students **publish** their final drafts on the writing templates and draw their bunny in the box. (If students need more writing lines, photocopy additional pages, or staple lined paper to the template.)
- Invite students to **create** construction paper bunny ears and glue them to the top of their paper and glue a cotton ball at the bottom for the tail.
- **Display** student work on a bulletin board titled *Bunny Tales*.

TEACHING HINTS/EXTENSIONS

- Read aloud *The Tale of Peter Rabbit* by Beatrix Potter (Frederick Warne). Encourage students to write a tale about Peter Rabbit getting into other mischief.
- Invite capable upper-grade, middle-school, or high-school students to assist you during reading and writing time. Have them help students by providing ideas, modeling sentences, and assisting with spelling and dictation.
- Set up a Beatrix Potter learning center with all her beloved stories. Read aloud the stories, and discuss the similarities and differences. Create a chart to keep track of the characters and their adventures.
- Have students complete one or more of these writing prompts in a journal:
  - ✔ Write a story about a lost bunny.
  - ✔ Write a story about a bunny that got into trouble.
  - ✔ Write about a bunny that went to school.

Bunny Shirt

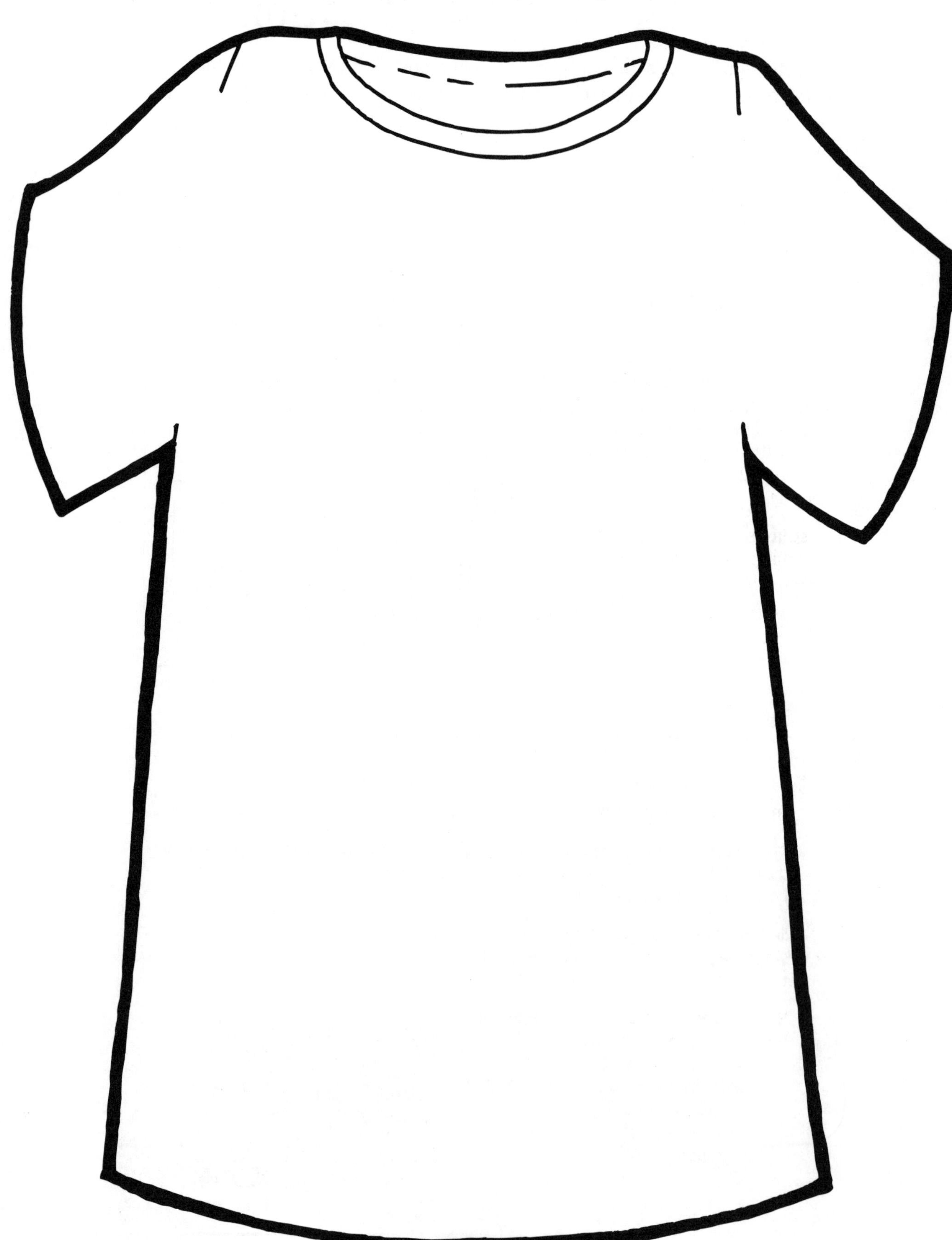

Name ______________________________ Date ______________________

Bunny Word Recognition

Directions: Fill in the bubble next to the word that best describes the picture.

- ◉ blue
- ○ bunny
- ○ boy

- ○ teeth
- ◉ too
- ○ time

- ○ whiskers
- ○ why
- ◉ wise

- ○ yes
- ○ eyes
- ◉ I

- ◉ nose
- ○ nice
- ○ near

- ◉ ears
- ○ eat
- ○ am

- ○ tail
- ○ tall
- ◉ take

- ◉ blue
- ○ boy
- ○ body

Name ______________________ Date ______________________

Kangaroo Chaos

Preparation

Read aloud books about kangaroos.

- *Elmer and the Kangaroo* by David McKee (HarperCollins)
- *Jump, Kangaroo, Jump!* by Stuart J. Murphy (HarperTrophy)
- *Kangaroo Island: A Story of an Australian Mallee Forest* by Deirdre Langeland (Nature Conservancy)

Collect pictures of kangaroos and scenes from Australia.

Gather three pieces of chart paper.

Make copies of these reproducibles.

- Kangaroo Word Recognition (page 60) transparency, class set of photocopies
- Kangaroo Brainstorm (page 61) transparency, class set of photocopies
- Kangaroo Shape Book (page 62) class set of photocopies on brown construction paper
- rubric (page 9) class set of photocopies

Setting the Stage

Tell students that a setting is the place where a story happens. Explain that settings are often very important to stories. For example, ask students if *Goldilocks and the Three Bears* would work if the story was set in an airplane. Review the books about kangaroos you read during the preceding week. Ask students to describe the setting of each story. Record their responses on the board or on a piece of chart paper. Invite the class to play a game. Name an animal (e.g., whale), and ask the class to identify where it lives (e.g., ocean). Use kangaroo as the last animal.

OBJECTIVE

The student will write sentences that describe the setting where a kangaroo lives.

CRITICAL COMPONENTS

- Each sentence and each proper noun begin with a capital letter.
- Each sentence ends with the correct punctuation.
- Sentences include specific details that describe a setting.

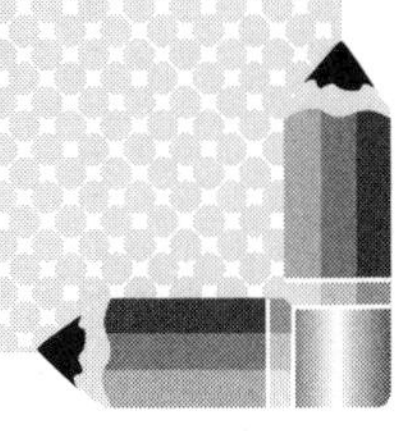

Instructional Input

1 Display the pictures of kangaroos and Australia you collected. Lead a discussion about kangaroos. Record information shared by students on a piece of chart paper.

2 Tell the class that kangaroos are native to Australia and that they hop around parks, on the roads, and even near people! Explain that kangaroos can be bothersome animals and can get into trouble. Invite students to think of a funny setting for a kangaroo character to have an adventure. For example, the kangaroo could hop into a museum and surprise people, hop into a school and enter a classroom, or go grocery shopping.

3 Listen to several ideas, and invite the class to vote on a setting. Then, have the class help you write sentences or a paragraph that describes the setting on another piece of chart paper. Encourage students to help you underline the setting in the first sentence and details about the setting in following sentences. Use the example as a guide.

> Kanga Kangaroo hopped into the <u>Alpha Beta Grocery Store</u>. She was amazed at all of the <u>food</u> on the shelves. There was cereal and bread. There were fruits and <u>vegetables</u>. There were <u>meats and milk</u>. Food was everywhere! Kanga Kangaroo grabbed a <u>grocery cart</u> and started to shop.

Guided Practice

1 Give each student a Kangaroo Word Recognition reproducible. Invite volunteers to identify the picture in each box. Say several sentences about kangaroos. For example, say *A kangaroo is large. A kangaroo is brown. I have never seen a kangaroo.* Tell students to fill in the bubble next to the word that best describes the picture.

2 Display the Kangaroo Word Recognition overhead transparency. Review the correct answers, and have students circle them.

3 Invite each student to think of a funny setting for a kangaroo to have an adventure (e.g., in a car, on the moon, in a large purse), and record each idea on another piece of chart paper.

4 Display the Kangaroo Brainstorm overhead transparency. Read aloud the example, and explain that once an author chooses a setting for a story, he or she must then think of at least three details about the setting so the reader knows what it looks like.

5 Invite the class to vote on a setting from the list you recorded. Have them help you write details about that setting on the transparency. Repeat this process for two or three settings or until students seem comfortable with creating a setting and details about it.

6 Invite students to help you write sentences or a paragraph about one of the settings you recorded on the transparency.

Independent Practice

1 Give each student a Kangaroo Brainstorm reproducible. Have students choose a setting from the list you recorded during Guided Practice or create their own. Encourage students to write as many details as they can about the setting. If they want to write more than three details, have students write them on the back of the reproducible or on a separate piece of paper.

2 Invite students to use these details to write several sentences or a paragraph about the setting. Remind them to write that the main character, a kangaroo, is in this setting.

3 Have students revise and edit their rough draft and then use the rubric to evaluate their writing.

Presentation

- Have students **publish** their final drafts on lined paper. Have them assemble the Kangaroo Shape Book reproducibles. Invite students to roll up their papers and place them in the "pouches."

- **Display** the shape books on a bulletin board titled *Hopping to New Places.*

TEACHING HINTS/EXTENSIONS

- Invite students to expand their settings into short stories. Teach them to develop characters and a beginning, middle, and ending with a problem and solution.

- Set up a kangaroo learning center. Write key vocabulary words on kangaroo-shaped cards. Have students practice reading the words with a partner and using the words in sentences.

- Have students use modeling dough or clay to create a map of Australia. Invite them to place Australian animals made from construction paper on the maps.

- Have students complete one or more of these writing prompts in a journal:
  - ✔ Describe a setting in which a dog is at the top of a tall palm tree.
  - ✔ Write about a setting in which a giraffe is stranded on a desert island.
  - ✔ Describe a setting in which a butterfly is alone in an arctic storm.

Name ______________________ Date ______________________

Kangaroo Word Recognition

Directions: Fill in the bubble next to the word that best describes the picture.

○ keep
○ kite
○ kangaroo

○ tell
○ tail
○ tall

○ happy
○ hop
○ hope

○ brown
○ blue
○ big

○ fur
○ fine
○ fee

○ pouch
○ pot
○ pond

○ smile
○ smell
○ smear

○ road
○ rock
○ rat

Name ______________________ Date ______________________

Kangaroo Brainstorm

EXAMPLE

Setting
The kangaroo is on the moon.

Detail: The moon is round and has craters.

Detail: The kangaroo lands in a rocket ship that looks like the Apollo.

Detail: The kangaroo sees a colony and discovers life on the moon.

Setting

____

____

Detail: ______________________

____

Detail: ______________________

____

Detail: ______________________

____

Kangaroo Shape Book

Directions: Cut out the kangaroo and its pouch. Staple the bottom and sides of the pouch to the kangaroo. Roll up your paper. Use a paper clip to keep it rolled up. Place it in the pouch.

Billy the Bear

Preparation

Read aloud books about bears.

- *Big Bad Bruce* by Bill Peet (Houghton Mifflin)
- *Lost* by David McPhail (Econo-Clad Books)
- *Where's My Teddy?* by Jez Alborough (Candlewick Press)

Gather chart paper.

Make copies of these reproducibles.

- Bear Word Recognition (page 66) transparency, class set of photocopies
- Bear Brainstorm (page 67) transparency, class set of photocopies
- Bear Story (page 68) transparency
- Bear Pattern (page 69) class set of photocopies on brown construction paper
- rubric (page 9) class set of photocopies

Setting the Stage

Review the books about bears you read during the preceding week. For each story, ask *What was the problem in the story? Who had the problem? What was the solution? How did the story work out?* Encourage students to also discuss and answer these questions about well-known stories such as *Little Red Riding Hood* or *The Three Little Pigs.*

OBJECTIVE

The student will write a story about a bear that includes a problem and a solution.

CRITICAL COMPONENTS

- The story includes a problem and a solution.
- Each sentence and each proper noun begin with a capital letter.
- Each sentence ends with the correct punctuation.

Instructional Input

1 Give each student a Bear Word Recognition reproducible. Invite volunteers to identify the picture in each box. Say several sentences about the bear body part. For example, say *A bear has sharp teeth. Its teeth are white. I don't want to get bitten by its teeth.* Tell students to fill in the bubble next to the word that best describes the picture.

2 Display the Bear Word Recognition overhead transparency. Review the correct answers, and have students circle them.

3 Ask students why stories have problems and solutions. Explain that good stories include interesting problems to keep the reader involved in the story. Challenge students to think of a story that does not have a problem and solution. Invite students to suggest stories, and discuss the plot to show them that every story has both.

4 Ask students to brainstorm different problems a bear might have (e.g., gets lost in the woods, is not able to find enough food to eat, gets arrested by a forest ranger for scaring campers), and record their responses on chart paper.

5 Invite students to think of an interesting solution for each problem. Record several ideas next to each problem.

Possible Problems	Possible Solutions
1. lost in the woods	• finds a trail back home • sniffs the wind and detects the presence of his mother • runs into a little boy who helps
2. can't find enough to eat	• finds a tree filled with honey • goes fishing in the lake • finds a wonderful berry bush

Guided Practice

1 Display the Bear Brainstorm overhead transparency and the list of possible problems and solutions you recorded in Instructional Input. Read aloud the example, and invite students to think of another problem that a bear character could have. Have the class vote on a problem to develop into a story, and record it on the transparency. Encourage volunteers to think of three solutions to the problem, and record them on the transparency.

2 Display the Bear Story overhead transparency. Read aloud the story with the blanks. Reread the story, and invite students to help you fill in the blanks with the problem and one or more of the solutions from the Bear Brainstorm transparency. Read aloud the completed story.

Independent Practice

1 Give each student a Bear Brainstorm reproducible. Have students choose a problem from the list you recorded in Instructional Input or think of their own. Encourage students to write as many possible solutions as they can. If they want to write more than three, have students write them on the back of the reproducible or on a separate piece of paper.

2 Invite students to use the information they wrote on the reproducible to write a story about a bear. Give a Bear Story reproducible to students who are more comfortable using the outline provided than writing a story on their own.

3 Have students revise and edit their rough draft and then use the rubric to evaluate their writing.

Presentation

- Have students **publish** their final drafts on several pieces of white lined paper cut to fit on the Bear Pattern reproducible body piece.

- Have students **create** bears from the Bear Pattern reproducibles. Have them use five brass fasteners to connect the body parts.
- **Display** student work on a bulletin board titled *Beary Good Stories.*

TEACHING HINTS/EXTENSIONS

- Read aloud *Goldilocks and the Three Bears: Bears Should Share (Another Point of View)* by Alvin Granowsky (Steck-Vaughn). Draw a Venn diagram on a piece of chart paper, and have students chart the similarities and differences between this story and the original Goldilocks and the Three Bears story.
- Host a "teddy bear picnic" in your classroom. Invite students to bring their favorite teddy bear to school and share information about it. Then, have students write stories using their own teddy bear as the main character.
- Cut out magazine or newspaper pictures that illustrate a problem. Have students write about solutions to the problems.
- Have students complete one or more of these writing prompts in a journal:
  - ✔ Write about twin baby bears. Describe the problem they have finding food and a solution to the problem.
  - ✔ Write a story about a bear that wants to meet a new friend. Tell about the problem it has finding a new friend and how it solves the problem.
  - ✔ Write a story about a mama and papa bear that have a flood in their cave during a rainstorm. What will they do?

Name Michelle Date

Bear Word Recognition

Directions: Fill in the bubble next to the word that best describes the picture.

◉ big ○ bear ○ bug	○ fur ○ for ◉ fine
◉ claw ○ clue ○ clip	○ arm ○ ape ◉ art
◉ teeth ○ team ○ this	○ leap ◉ leg ○ let
○ pain ◉ paws ○ pear	 ◉ boy ○ brave ○ body

Name ______________________________ Date ____________________

Bear Brainstorm

EXAMPLE

Problem
The bear cub scares a camper and gets arrested by a forest ranger.

Possible Solution: Uncle Harry, a bear, helps the cub escape.

Possible Solution: The bear cub goes to trial and is found not guilty.

Possible Solution: The forest ranger feels sorry for the cub and lets it go free.

Problem

____

____

Possible Solution: ______________________________

____

Possible Solution: ______________________________

____

Possible Solution: ______________________________

____

Name ____________________ Date ____________________

Bear Story

Once upon a time, there lived a bear named ____________________.

He had a friend named Michelle. Together they

____
(describe the problem)

____________________.

So, ____________________
(describe the solution)

____

____________________.

Bear Pattern

arm

head

arm

Attach arm here.

Attach leg here.

Attach head here.

Attach leg here.

Attach arm here.

body

leg

leg

A Whale of a Tale

Preparation

Read aloud books about whales.

- *A First Look at Whales* by Millicent E. Selsam and Joyce Hunt (Walker and Company)
- *A Garden of Whales* by Maggie Steincrohn Davis (Camden House)
- *Shh! The Whale is Smiling* by Josephine Nobisso (Gingerbread House)

Gather a world map that shows the oceans.

Prepare a video clip that includes a short scene of whales swimming in the ocean. Arrange to have a television and VCR in the classroom.

Make copies of these reproducibles.
- Tale of Willy and Lee (page 73) transparency
- Whale Word Recognition (page 74) transparency, class set of photocopies
- Whale Plot (page 75) transparency, class set of photocopies
- Whale Shape Book (page 76) transparency, class set of photocopies
- rubric (page 9) class set of photocopies

OBJECTIVE

The student will write a story about whales that includes a beginning, middle, and ending.

CRITICAL COMPONENTS

- The story includes characters, a setting, a problem, and a solution.
- The story has a beginning, middle, and ending.
- Each sentence and each proper noun begin with a capital letter.
- Each sentence ends with the correct punctuation.

Setting the Stage

Show a short video clip of whales swimming in the ocean. Ask students what the whales did, where they were, and what kinds of experiences they were having. Discuss whether students think it looked like the whales were having fun swimming in the ocean and whether they think it would be scary to swim in the middle of the ocean. Encourage students to explain their reasons. Invite them to share experiences they have had swimming in the ocean, lakes, rivers, and pools. Ask what kinds of rules their parents have taught them about swimming and why they are important.

Instructional Input

1 Display the Tale of Willy and Lee overhead transparency, which tells the story of two whales and an experience they had swimming and playing in the ocean. Read aloud the poem with the blanks. Reread the poem, and invite the class to help you fill in the blanks. Tell students that the word that belongs in the blank must rhyme with the last word in line two of the stanza. (Underlining the last word in line two of each stanza may help students.) Record several responses for each blank, and circle the word that the class votes on as the one that fits best.

2 Ask students to answer the following comprehension questions about the poem: *Who were the main characters? What were their names? What kind of characters were they? Where did they live? What happened to them in the beginning, middle, and ending? What was the problem? What was the solution? What lesson did they learn?* Point out that the beginning of the story introduces the setting and characters, the problem occurs in the middle of the story, and the ending of the story presents the solution to the problem.

3 Give each student a Whale Word Recognition reproducible. Invite volunteers to identify the picture in each box. Say several sentences about the picture such as *A whale lives in the sea. It hunts in the sea. It swims in the sea.* Tell students to fill in the bubble next to the word that best describes the picture.

4 Display the Whale Word Recognition overhead transparency. Review the correct answers, and have students circle them.

Guided Practice

1 Tell students that they will be writing stories about whales after the class writes one together. Invite students to brainstorm names for whale characters, and record two to four names on the board. Show students a world map, and point out the oceans. Invite the class to choose an ocean for the setting of the story. Have students think of a problem the whales will have (e.g., they are hungry and looking for dinner, one has a broken tooth, they crash into a boat). Select volunteers to suggest solutions for each problem. Record all the ideas on the board, and invite the class to vote on one problem and solution.

2 Display the Whale Plot overhead transparency. Review what information needs to be in the beginning (introduce setting and characters), middle (problem occurs), and ending (problem is solved).

3 Invite students to help you record information for the story in each whale. Encourage them to state information in complete sentences, and record the information in complete sentences. (Don't write the story. Just record ideas about what will happen in each section.)

4 Invite the class to help you use the information you recorded on the Whale Plot transparency to write a story. Model how to transfer the information from the whale sections into a complete story on the Whale Shape Book overhead transparency.

Independent Practice

1 Give each student a Whale Plot reproducible. Encourage students to think of whale character names, choose an ocean for the setting, and decide on a problem and a solution. Encourage them to fill in each whale with as many details as they can. This will help them turn the information into a story.

2 Invite students to use the information they recorded on the reproducible to write their story about whales.

3 Have students revise and edit their rough draft and then use the rubric to evaluate their writing.

Presentation

- Have students **publish** their stories on the Whale Shape Book reproducibles. (If students need more writing lines, photocopy additional pages, or have students trace the whale shape on lined paper.)
- Have students **create** front and back covers for their shape book by cutting out the whale shape, tracing it on construction paper, and cutting out their tracings. Then, have them staple all their pages together to make individual books.
- Encourage students to **share** their stories with the class or in small groups.

TEACHING HINTS/EXTENSIONS

- Invite students to make papier-mâché whales. Mix 1 part flour to 1 part water, and stir together. Blow up balloons for the bodies. Have students cover the balloons with one layer of newspaper strips dipped in papier-mâché mix. Cut empty toilet paper rolls in half the long way so you have two long strips. Tape them together in the shape of a "T" to make a tail. Have students tape the tail to the whale body and then use blank white strips of paper to cover the whole whale with a second layer of papier-mâché. Invite students to paint the whales, and then display them.

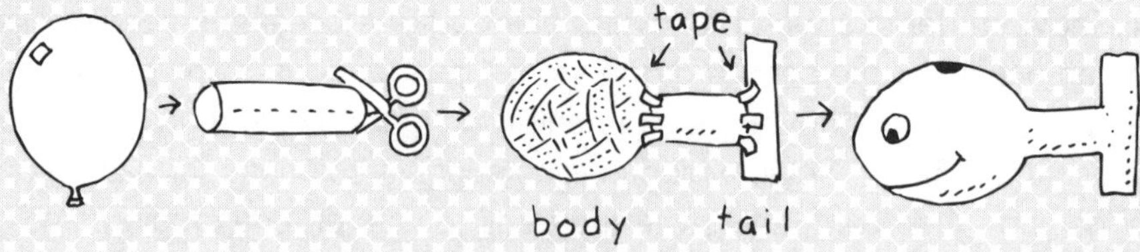

- Create a bulletin board titled *Wonderful Whales*. Display maps of oceans, posters of whales, and illustrations of whales. Place books about whales, including student-authored whale stories, just below the bulletin board.
- Invite students to write short stories about another ocean animal such as an octopus, a dolphin, or a crab. Remind them to include a beginning, middle, and ending. Encourage them to create a shape book for their writing.
- Have students complete one or more of these writing prompts in a journal:
  - ✔ Write a story about a whale and a boy who had an adventure.
  - ✔ Write a story about a fisherman and a whale that surprised each other.
  - ✔ Write a story about two whales that found a big surprise.

Tale of Willy and Lee

Directions: Fill in each blank with a word that rhymes with the last word in line two of the stanza.

Long ago,
In the open sea,
Lived a whale named Willy
And a whale named Lee.

They swam and played
And splashed about.
They jumped and dove
And blew their ______________.

Then a storm blew in
And the sky turned gray.
And suddenly they knew
They'd lost their ______________.

They began to cry.
They began to spout.
They began to scream.
They began to ______________.

"Help us! Help us!"
They did call.
"We do not know
where we are at ______________!"

Their mother came
And they were glad.
But she was scared
And also ______________.

"Do not play
So far away.
Swim and splash,
But do not ______________."

"I love you both,
my Willy and Lee.
You are my children,
My ______________."

"But as you swim,
Stay close at hand.
Keep one eye on me
And one on ______________."

Name ______________________________ Date ______________________

Whale Word Recognition

Directions: Fill in the bubble next to the word that best describes the picture.

○ let
○ land
○ luck

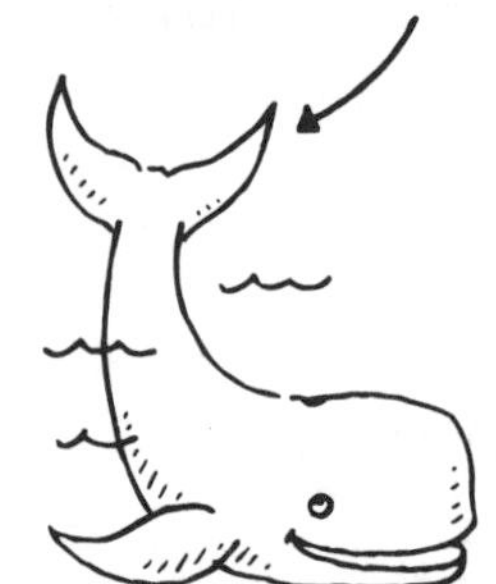

○ tail
○ toss
○ time

○ sea
○ saw
○ sit

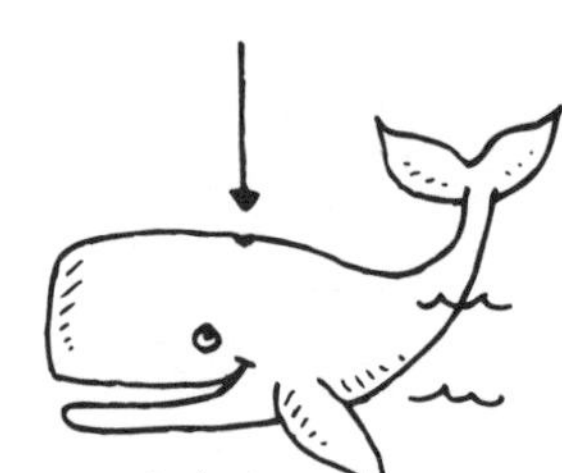

○ blowhole
○ blue
○ blow

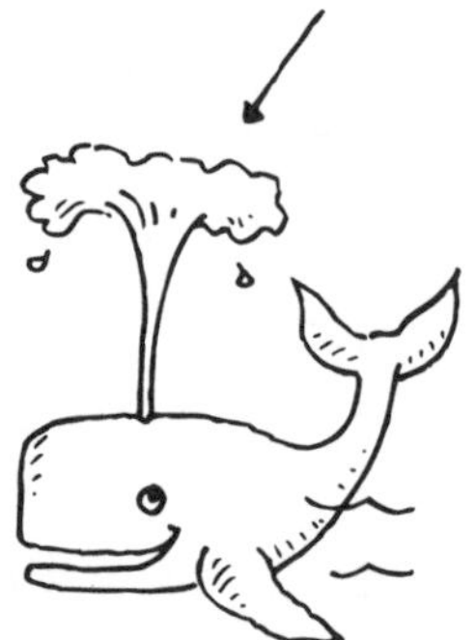

○ spot
○ spit
○ spout

○ teeth
○ tea
○ to

○ whale
○ why
○ what

○ don't
○ down
○ dive

Name ______________________________ Date ____________________

Whale Plot

Beginning

Middle

Ending

Whale Shape Book

Lionnel the Lion

Preparation

Read aloud stories about lions.

- *Eli* by Bill Peet (Houghton Mifflin)
- *Johnny Lion's Book* by Edith Thacher Hurd (HarperCollins)
- *A Lion Named Shirley Williamson* by Bernard Waber (Houghton Mifflin)

Gather three different colored overhead pens and chart paper.

Write *Narrator, Lionnel Lion*, and *Larry Lion* on sentence strips or index cards, and attach yarn to them to create name tag necklaces.

Make copies of these reproducibles.
- Lion Dialogue (page 80) transparency
- Lion Word Recognition (page 81) transparency, class set of photocopies
- Dialogue Frame (page 82) transparency, two class sets of photocopies
- Lion Puppet Pattern (page 83) teacher photocopy on orange construction paper, teacher photocopy and class set of photocopies on yellow construction paper
- rubric (page 9) class set of photocopies

Create two lion puppets with the Lion Puppet Pattern (page 83).

Setting the Stage

Introduce the two lion puppets. Invite students to interact with the puppets by talking with them and asking them questions. In the middle of this dialogue, have the puppets notice each other, meet, and become acquainted. After a few minutes of dialogue between the puppets, have them say good-bye to the class, and put them away.

OBJECTIVE

The student will write sentences about lions that include character dialogue.

CRITICAL COMPONENTS

- Quotation marks are used to identify words spoken by characters.
- Each sentence and each proper noun begin with a capital letter.
- Each sentence ends with the correct punctuation.

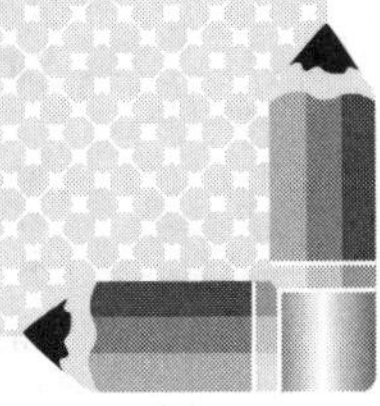

Instructional Input

1 Ask the class if they heard the puppets talking to each other and what kinds of things they said to each other. Explain that when people or animals talk to one another, it is called dialogue.

2 Take out the two lion puppets. Display the Lion Dialogue overhead transparency. Have the lion puppets read the dialogue while you read the part of the narrator. Then, invite three students to read aloud the dialogue as they wear the appropriate name tag necklaces. Encourage additional groups of students to read aloud the dialogue.

3 Invite three volunteers to take turns using three different colored overhead pens to underline the words each character said in the dialogue.

4 Ask the class if they notice any little marks that are unusual on the dialogue. Most likely, they will notice the quotation marks. Ask why they think those little marks are there. Explain that they are called quotation marks and are placed around the words that are said by a person, an animal, or a character.

Guided Practice

1 Give each student a Lion Word Recognition reproducible. Invite volunteers to identify the picture in each box. Say several sentences about lions. For example, say *Male lions have a mane. A mane is furry. A mane is yellow, orange, or brown.* Tell students to fill in the bubble next to the word that best describes the picture.

2 Display the Lion Word Recognition overhead transparency. Review the correct answers, and have students circle them.

3 Ask students to brainstorm different types of adventures two lions could have in a jungle (e.g., they go searching for a magical lake, they find an object next to a tree, they climb a tree). Record their ideas on a piece of chart paper.

4 Display the Dialogue Frame overhead transparency. Ask the class to choose names for the lions and an adventure for them to have. Have the class help you write a dialogue about the lions' adventure. Take out the two lion puppets, and have them read the dialogue while you read the part of the narrator.

5 Erase the dialogue on the transparency, and invite the class to help you write another one or two dialogues. With each dialogue, rename the lions and change the adventure they have.

Independent Practice

1 Encourage students to choose an adventure from the list you recorded in Guided Practice or think of their own adventure. Invite students to meet with a partner or a small group to discuss the adventure they want their lions to have. Encourage students to talk about the dialogue before they write it to help them clarify what they want to happen and what they want their lions to talk about.

2 Give each student a Dialogue Frame reproducible. Invite students to write a rough draft of a dialogue between two lions. Ask them to only fill in the dialogue and not draw pictures in the boxes since this is only the rough draft.

3 Have students revise and edit their rough draft and then use the rubric to evaluate their writing.

Presentation

- Have students **publish** their final drafts on another copy of the Dialogue Frame reproducible.
- Invite students to **create** puppets using the Lion Puppet Pattern reproducibles and paper bags.
- Encourage students to **present** dialogues to the class in groups of three so that one student plays the narrator and two students use their lion puppets to read the lions' dialogue.

TEACHING HINTS/EXTENSIONS

- Use this activity as a springboard into a unit on puppets. Set up a puppet theater and a puppet-making center. Invite students to explore puppetry and create puppet shows.
- Create a 3-D jungle mural with twisted dark green butcher paper for vines and twisted brown paper bags for tree trunks. Have students add leaves and animals.

- Invite students to write stories about the adventures of jungle animals. Encourage them to incorporate dialogue.
- Have students complete one or more of these writing prompts in a journal:
  - ✔ Lazy Lion and Hardworking Lion meet in the jungle. Hardworking Lion is mad at Lazy Lion. What do they say to each other? Write a dialogue.
  - ✔ Lippa Lion and Lester Lion meet in the jungle. Lippa Lion wants to be a famous singer. Lester is Lippa's best friend. Write a dialogue about their plans.
  - ✔ Lilly Lion and Lucy Lion are sisters. One day Lucy gets hurt while they are walking in the jungle. Write a dialogue about how Lilly helps Lucy.

Lion Dialogue

Narrator: "Good morning boys and girls. I am glad you could be here. Please meet Lionnel Lion."

Lionnel: (Bows and takes applause.)

Narrator: "Please meet Larry Lion."

Larry: (Bows and takes applause.)

Narrator: We are in Africa, deep in a jungle. Lionnel Lion and Larry Lion have just met.

Lionnel: "Hi. What's your name?"

Larry: "My name is Larry Lion. What's your name?"

Lionnel: "My name is Lionnel Lion."

Larry: "How old are you?"

Lionnel: "I am six years old. How old are you?"

Larry: "I am seven years old."

Lionnel: "Do you want to be friends?"

Larry: "Yes. I need a friend. I have been very lonely here in the jungle."

Lionnel: "Okay then. Come with me. I want to show you my favorite waterfall. We can splash and play there."

Larry: "That sounds fun. Let's go!"

Narrator: "That was the first time that Lionnel Lion and Larry Lion played together. They had a great time and became best friends for many years to come. The End."

Name ______________________________ Date ____________________

Lion Word Recognition

Directions: Fill in the bubble next to the word that best describes the picture.

- ○ love
- ○ lion
- ○ list

- ○ claws
- ○ cling
- ○ collect

- ○ mane
- ○ mom
- ○ moth

- ○ time
- ○ teeth
- ○ the

- ○ rain
- ○ roar
- ○ red

- ○ ferocious
- ○ for
- ○ fur

- ○ eyes
- ○ I
- ○ ever

- ○ jungle
- ○ jumping
- ○ judge

Name ______________________________ Date ______________________________

Dialogue Frame

Directions: Draw your lions in the first two boxes. Write their names. Draw your narrator in the third box.

Lion One	**Lion Two**	**Narrator**

Narrator: "Once upon a time, there lived two lions in a jungle. The first lion was named ______________________________ and the second lion was named ______________________________. Today, they are going on an adventure."

Lion One: "______________________________."

Lion Two: "______________________________."

Lion One: "______________________________."

Lion Two: "______________________________."

Lion One: "______________________________."

Lion Two: "______________________________."

Lion One: "______________________________."

Lion Two: "______________________________."

Lion One: "______________________________."

Lion Two: "______________________________."

Narrator: "The End. We hope you enjoyed our show!"

Lion Puppet Pattern

Directions: Cut out the pattern. Cut across the dotted line. Glue the top part of the lion's head on the top of a brown paper bag. Glue the bottom part of the lion's head to the bottom of the bag. Decorate your lion.

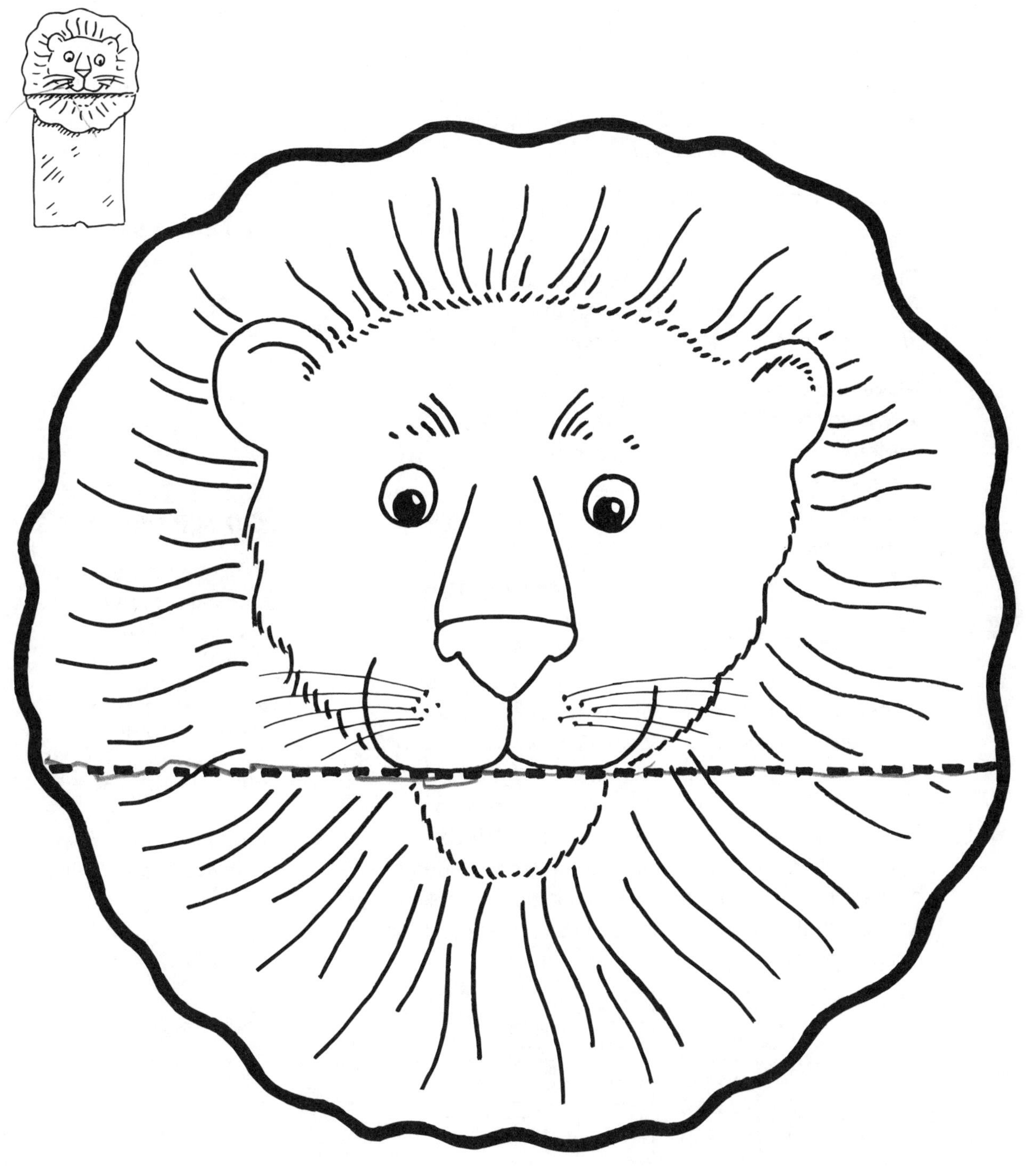

Monkey Business

Preparation

Read aloud books about mischievous monkeys.

- *Caps for Sale* by Esphyr Solbodkina (HarperCollins)
- *Curious George Makes Pancakes* by Margret & H. A. Rey (Houghton Mifflin)
- *Five Little Monkeys Sitting in a Tree* by Eileen Christelow (Clarion Books)

Gather chart paper and four different colored overhead pens.

Create a poster of the "Monkey Business" poem in Instructional Input and a chart with the headings *Title/Author, Plot, Problem, Solution,* and *Best Part.*

Make copies of these reproducibles.

- Monkey Story Frame (page 87) transparency
- Monkey Word Recognition (page 88) transparency, class set of photocopies
- Monkey Shape Book (page 89) class set of photocopies
- rubric (page 9) class set of photocopies

Setting the Stage

Review the books about monkeys you read during the preceding week. Ask students the following questions about each book: *What was the title of the book? Who was the author? What was the story about? What kind of problem did the main character have? What was the solution? What did you enjoy most about the story?* Record their responses on the chart you prepared. Have students brainstorm a word bank of words related to monkeys, and record the words on index cards, sentence strips, or chart paper.

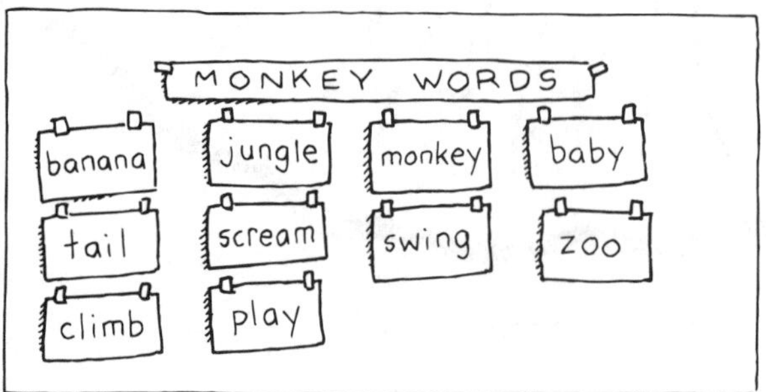

OBJECTIVE

The student will write a short story about two mischievous monkeys.

CRITICAL COMPONENTS

- The story includes characters, a setting, a problem, and a solution.
- Each sentence and each proper noun begin with a capital letter.
- Each sentence ends with the correct punctuation.

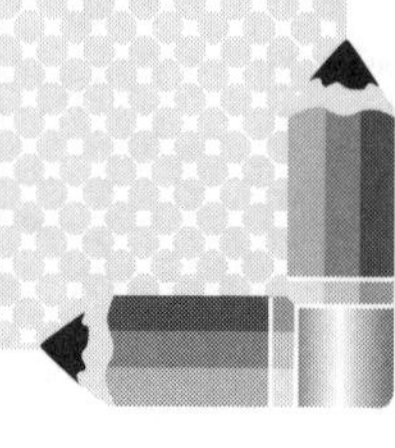

Instructional Input

1 Display the poster of the "Monkey Business" poem. Invite students to close their eyes and visualize a jungle filled with monkeys while you read aloud the poem. Encourage students to read aloud the poem as you reread it.

2 Ask students to think about what mischief two monkeys may get in while playing in the jungle. Give students 3 to 5 minutes to do a "sketch-to-stretch exercise" where they quickly draw what they are thinking. Encourage students to share their pictures. Record examples of mischief that monkeys may get in on a piece of chart paper.

Monkey Business

Trees so high
  and trees so low.
To the top
  the monkeys go.

They fight, they play,
  they dash about.
They scream, they cry,
  they laugh, they shout!

Monkeys high,
  monkeys low.
To the top
  the monkeys go!

3 Remind students that every good story has a problem and a solution. Explain that mischief that the monkey characters get into could be the problem of the story. Invite students to brainstorm ideas for problems and solutions for a story about monkeys, and record their ideas on the piece of chart paper.

Problem	Solution
The monkey tickled his friend and the friend got mad. They had a big fight.	Later, the monkeys shared a banana and made up.
A monkey fell from a tree and got stuck between two branches.	The monkey stayed in the tree for three days until a firefighter rescued it.

4 Display the Monkey Story Frame overhead transparency. Read aloud the story with the blanks. Invite the class to use one of the problems and solutions you recorded to write a story. Have students help you develop the story, and record it on the transparency. Invite volunteers to take turns using four different colored overhead pens to underline the characters, setting, problem, and solution.

Guided Practice

1 Give each student a Monkey Word Recognition reproducible. Invite volunteers to identify the picture in each box. Say several sentences using the word in the picture. For example, say *I saw a monkey eat a banana. A banana is yellow. A banana has a peel around it.* Tell students to fill in the bubble next to the word that best describes the picture.

2 Display the Monkey Word Recognition overhead transparency. Review the correct answers, and have students circle them.

3 Invite students to do a "think/pair/share exercise." Have them think of problems two monkeys may have in a jungle, find a partner, and share the information. Have students tell the class one idea that their partner shared with them. Add these ideas to the list you recorded in Instructional Input.

Independent Practice

1 Invite students to write a short story about two mischievous monkeys in the jungle. Encourage students to choose a problem and a solution from the list you recorded in Instructional Input, use the one they drew in the sketch-to-stretch exercise in Instructional Input, or think of a new idea. Give a Monkey Story Frame reproducible to students who feel more comfortable using the outline provided than writing a story on their own.

2 Have students revise and edit their rough draft and then use the rubric to evaluate their writing.

Presentation

- Have students **publish** their final drafts on the Monkey Shape Book reproducibles. (If students need more writing lines, photocopy additional pages, or have students trace the monkey shape on lined paper.)
- Have students **create** front and back covers for their shape book by cutting out the monkey shape, tracing it on construction paper, and cutting out their tracings. Then, have them staple all their pages together to make individual books.
- Encourage students to **share** their stories with the class or in small groups.
- **Display** the shape books in the classroom library.

TEACHING HINTS/EXTENSIONS

- Create a bulletin board titled *Monkey Business* with tree trunks made with twisted brown butcher paper or brown paper grocery bags. Pin large green butcher paper leaves on the tree. Invite students to hang their shape books in the trees.
- Use correction fluid to delete the writing lines on the Monkey Shape Book reproducible, and photocopy the revised reproducible on brown construction paper. Write a math problem on each monkey. Staple the monkeys on a bulletin board titled *Monkey Math*. Invite students to cut bananas from yellow construction paper, write the answers on them, and post their banana next to the monkey.
- Have students use the pattern in the following poem to create their own rhymes.

  Two little monkeys playing in a tree.
  One fell down and broke its knee.
  One monkey laughed and one monkey cried.
  One monkey smiled and one monkey sighed.
  Two little monkeys playing in a tree.
  Now they are as careful, as careful as can be!

- Have students complete one or more of these writing prompts in a journal:
  - ✔ Manny Monkey and May Monkey found an empty boat by the riverside. They got in and started to play. The boat began to sail away. What should they do?
  - ✔ Marla Monkey and Mattie Monkey were best friends until they got in a fight. What did they fight about? How did they solve their problem?
  - ✔ Gary Gorilla and Gregg Gorilla got lost in the jungle. Write about how they found their way home.

Monkey Story Frame

Once upon a time, there were two monkeys named

____________________ and ____________________.

These monkeys were walking in the jungle when ________________

____

____.

When that happened, they ____________________________

____

____.

Finally, ____

____

____.

Name ______________________________ Date ____________________

Monkey Word Recognition

Directions: Fill in the bubble next to the word that best describes the picture.

○ time
○ tea
○ tire

○ can
○ cave
○ cart

○ monkey
○ mom
○ man

○ river
○ run
○ rat

○ banana
○ ball
○ bath

○ eat
○ ear
○ eel

○ trap
○ toe
○ tree

○ cat
○ crib
○ cry

Monkey Shape Book

Mierelle

843

Creative Crocodile

Preparation

Read aloud stories about crocodiles.

- *The Bird Who Was Afraid to Clean the Crocodile's Teeth* by Paris Sandow and Taylor Brandon (Imperious)
- *The Enormous Crocodile* by Roald Dahl (Knopf)
- *Lyle, Lyle Crocodile* by Bernard Waber (Houghton Mifflin)

Gather a large poster of a crocodile.

Prepare a short video clip of a crocodile. Arrange to have a television and VCR in the classroom.

Create a chart with the headings *Characteristics, How the Crocodile Feels,* and *Exaggerated Response*.

Make copies of these reproducibles.

- Crocodile Word Recognition (page 93) transparency, class set of photocopies
- Crocodile Story (page 94) transparency, one photocopy for every two students
- Crocodile Shape Book (page 95) two or three class sets of photocopies
- rubric (page 9) class set of photocopies

Setting the Stage

Show a short video clip of a crocodile, and display a large poster of a crocodile. Review the books about crocodiles you read aloud during the preceding week, and then display them at the front of the classroom. Ask students to name the characteristics of crocodiles (e.g., has a long tail, big shiny teeth, and dry skin; lives in a swamp). Record their responses under "Characteristics" on the chart you prepared. Encourage students to tell about each characteristic in a sentence.

OBJECTIVE

The student will write a story about a crocodile that has an exaggerated problem.

CRITICAL COMPONENTS

- The story includes characters, a setting, an exaggerated problem, and a solution.
- Each sentence and each proper noun begin with a capital letter.
- Each sentence ends with the correct punctuation.

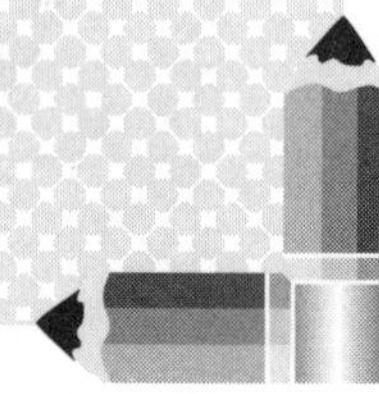

Instructional Input

1 Give each student a Crocodile Word Recognition reproducible. Invite volunteers to identify the picture in each box. Say several sentences using the word in the picture. For example, say *A boat can be small or big. I went on a boat in a swamp to see crocodiles. My dad owns a boat.* Tell students to fill in the bubble next to the word that best describes the picture.

2 Display the Crocodile Word Recognition overhead transparency. Review the correct answers, and have students circle them.

3 Invite students to brainstorm a word bank of words related to crocodiles, and record the words on a piece of chart paper, sentence strips, or index cards.

4 Explain that authors often write stories that are based on special characteristics of the animals or people in the story. Ask students to brainstorm how a crocodile character might feel about a characteristic it has and then to imagine an outrageously silly (exaggerated) response that could occur as a result. Record their ideas on the chart you prepared. Ask students if each characteristic is realistic for a crocodile, if each response is outrageously silly (exaggerated), and if the information you recorded could be used to write a story. Revise the information in the chart, as needed. (See the example below.)

Characteristics	How the Crocodile Feels	Exaggerated Response
has a long tail	feels shy about tail	The crocodile hides in the reeds every day until the sun goes down so no one sees its tail.
lives in a swamp	proud of how fast it swims	The crocodile swims so fast in the swamp that no one sees it pass the finish line in the swamp race each year.
has dry skin	feels itchy	It travels to towns around the world to find someone who can make a lotion so that its skin won't itch.

Guided Practice

1 Display the Crocodile Story overhead transparency. Read aloud the story with the blanks. Reread the story, and invite students to help you fill in the blanks with words from the reproducible and their own words. Read aloud the completed story, and then encourage students to reread it along with you.

2 Invite students to work with a partner to fill in the Crocodile Story reproducible. Give each pair a reproducible. If partners need help with vocabulary or spelling, have them refer to the word bank about crocodiles and the chart you recorded in Instructional Input.

3 Ask partners to read their story to the whole class or in small groups.

Independent Practice

1 Display the chart with crocodile characteristics on it. Ask the class to brainstorm additional characteristics of crocodiles, and record them under the chart or on the board.

2 Invite students to choose a characteristic from the list or think of a characteristic for the main character in the story they will write. Encourage each student to share that characteristic with the class.

3 Have students write a story about a crocodile. Remind them to write about the crocodile's characteristic and how the crocodile feels about it in the beginning of the story, to tell about the crocodile's response in the middle of the story, and to solve the crocodile's problem in the ending of the story. Give a Crocodile Story reproducible to students who feel more comfortable using the outline provided than writing a story on their own.

4 Have students revise and edit their rough draft and then use the rubric to evaluate their writing.

Presentation

- Have students **publish** their final drafts on two or three Crocodile Shape Book reproducibles.
- Have students **create** front and back covers for their shape book by cutting out the crocodile shape, tracing it on construction paper, and cutting out their tracings. Then, have them staple all their pages together to make individual books.
- Encourage students to **share** their shape books with a class of younger students.

TEACHING HINTS/EXTENSIONS

- Invite students to draw the shape of a crocodile on green construction paper. Have them cut out the shape and glue it to a craft stick or brown paper bag. Encourage students to use their puppets to share their stories with the class.
- Create a swamp mural. Display it on a classroom wall or in the school's hallway. Invite students to draw the crocodile in their story with its characteristic highlighted (e.g., large teeth, small tail) somewhere in the swamp.
- Draw a crocodile outline, and photocopy it on different colored paper. Cut out the shapes. Write a crocodile vocabulary word on each shape, and post the shapes on a bulletin board to create a word bank.

- Have students complete one or more of these writing prompts in a journal:
  - ✔ Candy the Crocodile loves sweets, but she eats too much. Tell about what happened to Candy when she visited the dentist.
  - ✔ Carlos the Crocodile loves to play sports. Write a story about the day he played football.
  - ✔ Colorful Crocodile is going to a party. She loves bright colors and patterns, so she wears a really colorful outfit. Describe her outfit and how the other crocodiles respond to it.

Name ______________________ Date ______________________

Crocodile Word Recognition

Directions: Fill in the bubble next to the word that best describes the picture.

○ crocodile ○ cracker ○ cream	○ ten ○ tear ○ tail
○ mud ○ mop ○ more	○ swamp ○ sweet ○ swallow
○ tail ○ tea ○ teeth	○ bone ○ ball ○ boat
○ I ○ eye ○ eat	○ play ○ plants ○ pick

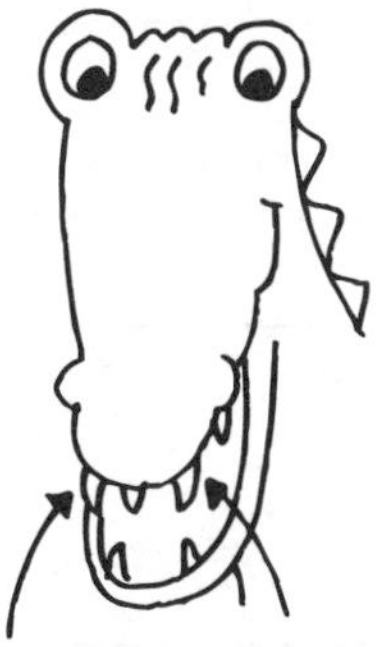

Crocodile Story

Once upon a time, there lived a crocodile named ________________.

There was a ________________ thing about this crocodile.
(funny, sad, great)

It had ________________________________
(a characteristic)

________________________________.

This made it feel ________________. In fact,
(embarrassed, shy, happy, sad, angry)

________________ was so ________________,
(name) (feeling)

that it ________________________________
(response)

____

____

________________________________.

Crocodile Shape Book

Hot Topic

Preparation

Read aloud books about the desert.

- *Desert Song* by Tony Johnston (Sierra Club)
- *Desert Trek: An Eye-Opening Journey Through the World's Driest Places* by Marie-Ange Le Rochais (Walker & Company)
- *Rattlesnake Dance* by Jim Arnosky (Putnam)

Gather chart paper and pictures of the desert.

Bring a small cactus plant to class.

Make copies of these reproducibles.

- Desert Word Recognition (page 99) transparency, class set of photocopies
- Desert Museum (page 100) transparency, class set of photocopies
- Cactus Shape Book (page 101) class set of photocopies
- rubric (page 9) class set of photocopies

Setting the Stage

Show students the cactus plant you brought and pictures of the desert. Ask if any of the students have a cactus plant in their yard or house. Write *cactus* on the board. (Talk about how you make the word plural: *cacti*.) Encourage students to talk about any experiences they have had visiting the desert or what they would see if they did visit one. Record their responses on a piece of chart paper. Invite students to read aloud the list.

Desert

- dry
- hot
- lizards
- snakes
- Arizona
- cactus
- lots of sand
- not a lot of rain
- over 100° F
- Grand Canyon
- cold at night

OBJECTIVE

The student will write sentences that tell about the desert.

CRITICAL COMPONENTS

- Sentences include facts about the desert.
- Each sentence and each proper noun begin with a capital letter.
- Each sentence ends with the correct punctuation.

Instructional Input

1 Give each student a Desert Word Recognition reproducible. Invite volunteers to identify the picture in each box. Say several sentences using the word in the picture. For example, say *I have a pet lizard. I named my lizard Boo Boo. A lizard lives in the desert.* Tell students to fill in the bubble next to the word that best describes the picture.

2 Display the Desert Word Recognition overhead transparency. Review the correct answers, and have students circle them.

3 Invite each student to say a sentence about the desert that includes one of the words from the reproducible. Encourage students to add details to their classmates' sentences.

4 Give each student a Desert Museum reproducible, and display the overhead transparency. Read aloud the story. Invite students to read along with you as you reread it. Have students underline words in the story that tell about the desert, and underline them on the transparency. Ask students to share what information Pete learned about the desert during his museum visit.

5 Read aloud the sentences at the bottom of the reproducible, and tell students to fill in the bubble next to each true statement about the desert and cross out the false statements. Fill in bubbles and cross out statements on the transparency.

Guided Practice

1 Invite students to do a "think/pair/share exercise." Have them think about everything they know about deserts, find a partner, and share the information.

2 Have students do a "sketch-to-stretch exercise." Ask them to draw a detailed picture of the desert that includes animals and plants. Invite students to share their picture with the whole class or in small groups. Collect the pictures to use in Independent Practice.

Independent Practice

1 Have students write several sentences about the desert. Encourage them to look at the picture they drew in Guided Practice and use the picture and the information about deserts you recorded in Setting the Stage to guide their writing.

2 Have students revise and edit their rough draft and then use the rubric to evaluate their writing.

Presentation

- Have students **publish** their final drafts on the Cactus Shape Book reproducibles. (If students need more writing lines, photocopy additional pages, or have them write on lined paper.)
- Have students **create** front and back covers for their shape book by cutting out the cactus shape, tracing it on construction paper, and cutting out their tracings. Then, have them staple all their pages together to make individual books.
- Encourage students to **share** their shape books in small groups.

TEACHING HINTS/EXTENSIONS

- Invite students to act out the following poem about a desert snake.

Sammy the Desert Snake

Sammy is a slithering snake. (*wiggle the body*)
He lays in the sand where it's hot and he bakes. (*lay on the carpet*)
He wiggles under rocks to catch a snack. (*wiggle then snap arms with a clap*)
(*big voice*) Watch out! (*whisper*) He's sneaky. (*shake finger*) And that's a fact!

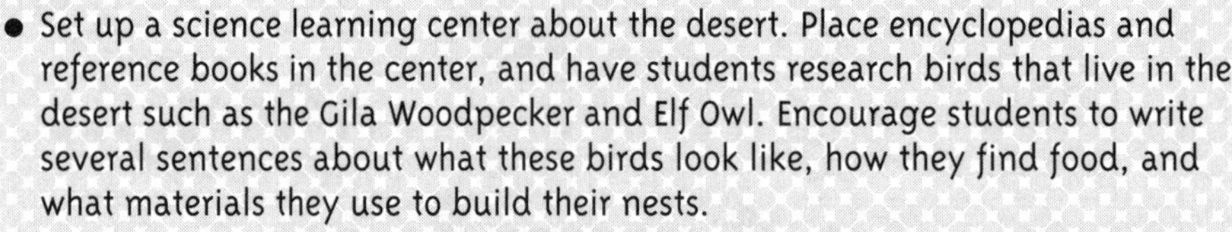

- Set up a science learning center about the desert. Place encyclopedias and reference books in the center, and have students research birds that live in the desert such as the Gila Woodpecker and Elf Owl. Encourage students to write several sentences about what these birds look like, how they find food, and what materials they use to build their nests.
- Read aloud a book about the desert such as *Sahara: Vanishing Cultures* by Jan Reynolds (Harcourt). Set up a social studies learning center. Invite students to color in the Sahara Desert on a map of Africa and draw a picture of a desert scene. Ask them to write several sentences about what life would be like if they lived in the Sahara Desert.
- Have students complete one or more of these writing prompts in a journal:
  - ✔ You are a tortoise that lives in the desert. Write about what you did today.
  - ✔ Describe the plants that live in the desert.
  - ✔ Imagine you are going on a trip to the desert. What will you pack in your suitcase?

Name ______________________ Date ______________________

Desert Word Recognition

Directions: Fill in the bubble next to the word that best describes the picture.

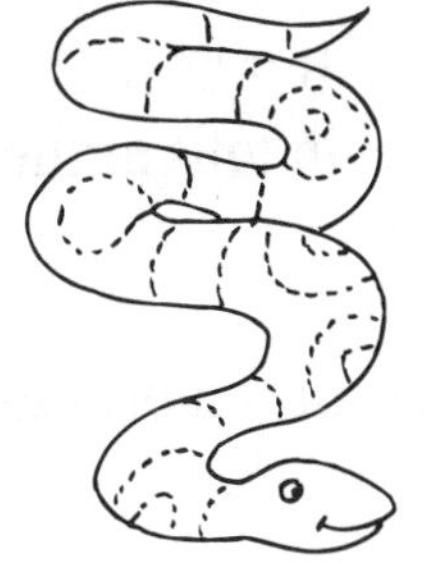

- ○ sand
- ○ shore
- ○ snake

- ○ desert
- ○ deep
- ○ deck

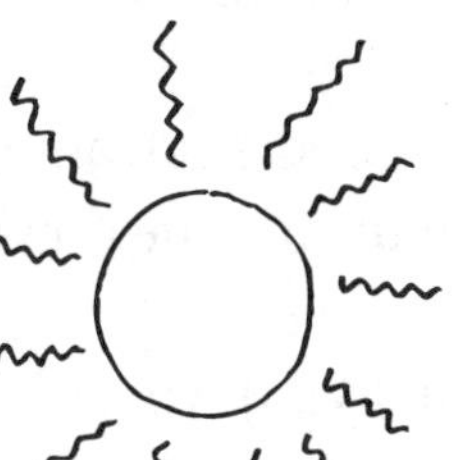

- ○ hop
- ○ hot
- ○ hat

- ○ cat
- ○ chicken
- ○ cactus

- ○ sand
- ○ sack
- ○ sad

- ○ lime
- ○ lizard
- ○ lamp

- ○ rat
- ○ race
- ○ rain

- ○ stop
- ○ spider
- ○ spray

Name ________________________________ Date ________________________

Desert Museum

Pete and his family are visiting a desert museum for the day. "Ouch!" cried Pete. "That cactus needle is sharp!"

"Cactus spines are very prickly," the museum guide told Pete, "so be careful. Did you know that those spines are there for a reason?"

"I guess they would protect the cactus," said Pete.

"That's right. Those spines keep animals from eating the plant. But those spines also provide shade. The desert is very hot and dry. Not much rain falls in the desert. Sometimes years go by with no rain," said the museum guide.

"How does a cactus plant get water?" asked Pete.

"The desert gets cold at night. Those spines collect dew in the early morning, which provides the cactus with a little water," responded the guide.

"Where do the animals get water?" asked Pete.

"Desert animals must be able to live without much water. Most of them get the water they need from the plants or insects they eat," the museum guide told Pete.

"But how do they keep cool?" questioned Pete.

"Animals such as snakes and lizards have tough skin to protect them from the heat. They hide in the sand or sleep in the shade of a rock or bush during the day," answered the guide.

"The desert sounds too hot and dry for me," said Pete. "I like living where it rains a lot!"

Directions: Fill in the bubble next to the true statements about the desert. Cross out the false statements about the desert.

○ The desert is very hot and dry.
○ The desert is nice and cool.

○ It rains every day.
○ Years can go by with no rain in the desert.

○ The desert gets cold at night.
○ The desert stays very hot at night.

○ Desert animals need lots of water.
○ Desert animals live without much water.

○ Desert animals hide in the sand to stay cool.
○ Desert animals hide in the water to stay cool.

○ Desert animals like to run in the sun.
○ Desert animals sleep in the shade when it is hot.

○ A cactus has sharp spines.
○ A cactus plant is fun to touch.

Cactus Shape Book

Cars, Buildings, People

Preparation

Read aloud books about cities.

- *The Little House* by Virginia Lee Burton (Houghton Mifflin)
- *Next Stop!* by Sarah Ellis (Fitzhenry & Whiteside)
- *Red Light, Green Light, Mamma and Me* by Cari Best (Orchard Books)

Obtain a copy of *Town Mouse Country Mouse* by Jan Brett (Putnam).

Gather one file folder and a piece of string 20 inches (50 cm) long for the teacher and each student and two pieces of chart paper.

Make copies of these reproducibles.

- City Word Recognition (page 105) transparency, class set of photocopies
- Street and Car Cutouts (page 106) teacher photocopy and class set of photocopies on card stock
- Buildings and Park Cutouts (page 107) teacher photocopy and class set of photocopies on card stock
- rubric (page 9) class set of photocopies

Prepare a sample map of a city. (See Guided Practice.)

Setting the Stage

Read aloud *Town Mouse Country Mouse*. Ask students to imagine what they would see if they walked around a city or town (e.g., traffic, many buildings, lots of people). Invite them to imagine what they would see if they walked around the country (e.g., open land, more trees and plants, less people, less traffic). Encourage students to use complete sentences to tell about what things they would see and the places they would go in each location. Record their responses on a piece of chart paper to create city and country word banks. Discuss how the city is different from the country. Draw a Venn diagram on another piece of chart paper, and record similarities and differences between the city and country.

OBJECTIVE

The student will write several sentences that tell about the city.

CRITICAL COMPONENTS

- Sentences include facts about the city.
- Each sentence and each proper noun begin with a capital letter.
- Each sentence ends with the correct punctuation.

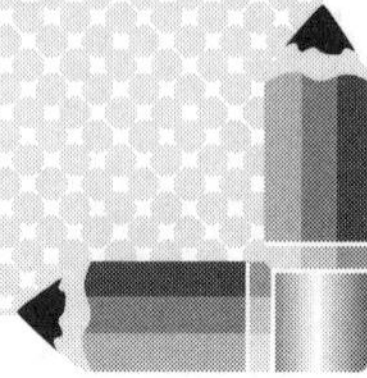

Instructional Input

1 Have the class play the game "Guess Where?" Choose a specific place such as a library. Tell students that you are thinking of a place in the city. Invite them to ask "yes" or "no" questions (e.g., *Is the place big? Is it outside?*). After the students identify your place, continue the game by inviting volunteers to take turns thinking of a place.

2 Give each student a City Word Recognition reproducible. Invite volunteers to identify the location in each box. Say several sentences about the location. For example, say *We are at school right now. We do not go to school on Saturday. This school is nice.* Tell students to fill in the bubble next to the name of the location.

3 Display the City Word Recognition overhead transparency. Review the correct answers, and have students circle them.

Guided Practice

1 Show students the sample map of a city you prepared. Give each student a file folder, string, crayons or markers, scissors, glue, a Street and Car Cutouts reproducible, and a Building and Park Cutouts reproducible.

2 Tell students to color the car, wheels, and street and then cut them out. Have students draw a dotted line down the center of the street to make two car lanes. Ask them to glue the wheels to the car and write their name on the car.

3 Have students hole-punch the tab of the file folder and the car and use string to tie the car to the folder. Invite them to glue the street to the inside of the file folder.

4 Read aloud the sentence starters on the Buildings and Park Cutouts reproducible. Tell students to complete each sentence. Encourage them to use the word bank you recorded in Setting the Stage or their own words. Have students cut out the park and buildings and glue them along the street inside of their file folder. Encourage students to create additional buildings to add to their city, if they finish early.

Independent Practice

1 Invite students to write several sentences about a nearby city, a city they have visited, or a city they would like to visit. Tell them to include details about what they will see, places they will go, and things they will do in the city. Encourage students to use the word bank and Venn diagram from Setting the Stage and the sentences they wrote in Guided Practice for ideas and vocabulary.

2 Have students revise and edit their rough draft and then use the rubric to evaluate their writing.

Presentation

- Have students **publish** their final drafts on white lined paper.
- **Display** students' sentences next to their maps on a bulletin board titled *Busy City Life.*

TEACHING HINTS/EXTENSIONS

- Review the hard and soft sounds of *c*. Draw a chart on the board with the headings *City* and *Country*. Invite students to think of words that begin with the letter *c* that could be found in the city or the country. Record each word under the correct heading. Ask students to circle words that begin with a soft *c* and draw a box around words that begin with a hard *c*.

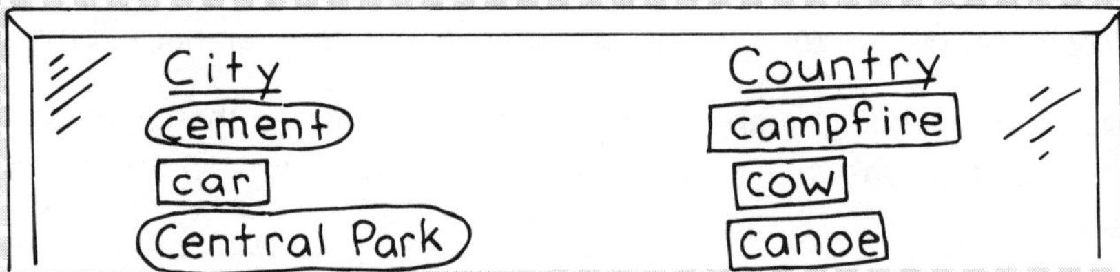

- Expand your class discussion about the city, and talk about the fact that a group of cities make up a county. Ask students if they know what county they live in. Continue the discussion to include state, country, continent, planet, solar system, and universe. Illustrate each category by showing students an appropriate map or picture.
- Invite the class to use the tune "The Wheels On the Bus Go Round and Round" to create a song about a city. Use the following verse and suggestions for additional verses as an example:

We go to the store to buy food, food, food,
Food, food, food,
Food, food, food.
We go to the store to buy food, food, food
In Los Angeles.

We go to a restaurant to eat and talk.
We go to the park to swing and slide.
We go to school to learn to read.
We go to the library to borrow books.

- Have students complete one or more of these writing prompts in a journal:
  - ✔ Write five or more sentences about the community you live in.
  - ✔ Write about a building or a park you would like to build in a city. Where will you build it? What will it look like?
  - ✔ Write about a trip to the country. Take an interesting form of transportation such as a horse or a hot air balloon to get there.

Name ______________________________ Date ____________________

City Word Recognition

Directions: Fill in the bubble next to the name of the location.

- ○ park
- ○ pot
- ○ pack

- ○ post office
- ○ porcupine
- ○ paper

- ○ sack
- ○ stop
- ○ store

- ○ prairie dog
- ○ park
- ○ police station

- ○ lamb
- ○ library
- ○ lock

- ○ fir tree
- ○ fish
- ○ fire station

- ○ school
- ○ shark
- ○ store

- ○ restaurant
- ○ rocket
- ○ rooster

Street and Car Cutouts

Directions: Cut out the street. Draw a line down the center to make two car lanes. Cut out the car and wheels. Glue the wheels to the car. Use a hole punch to make a hole in the tab of the file folder and in the top of the car. Write your name on the car. Use a piece of string to tie it to your file folder. Glue the street to the inside of the file folder.

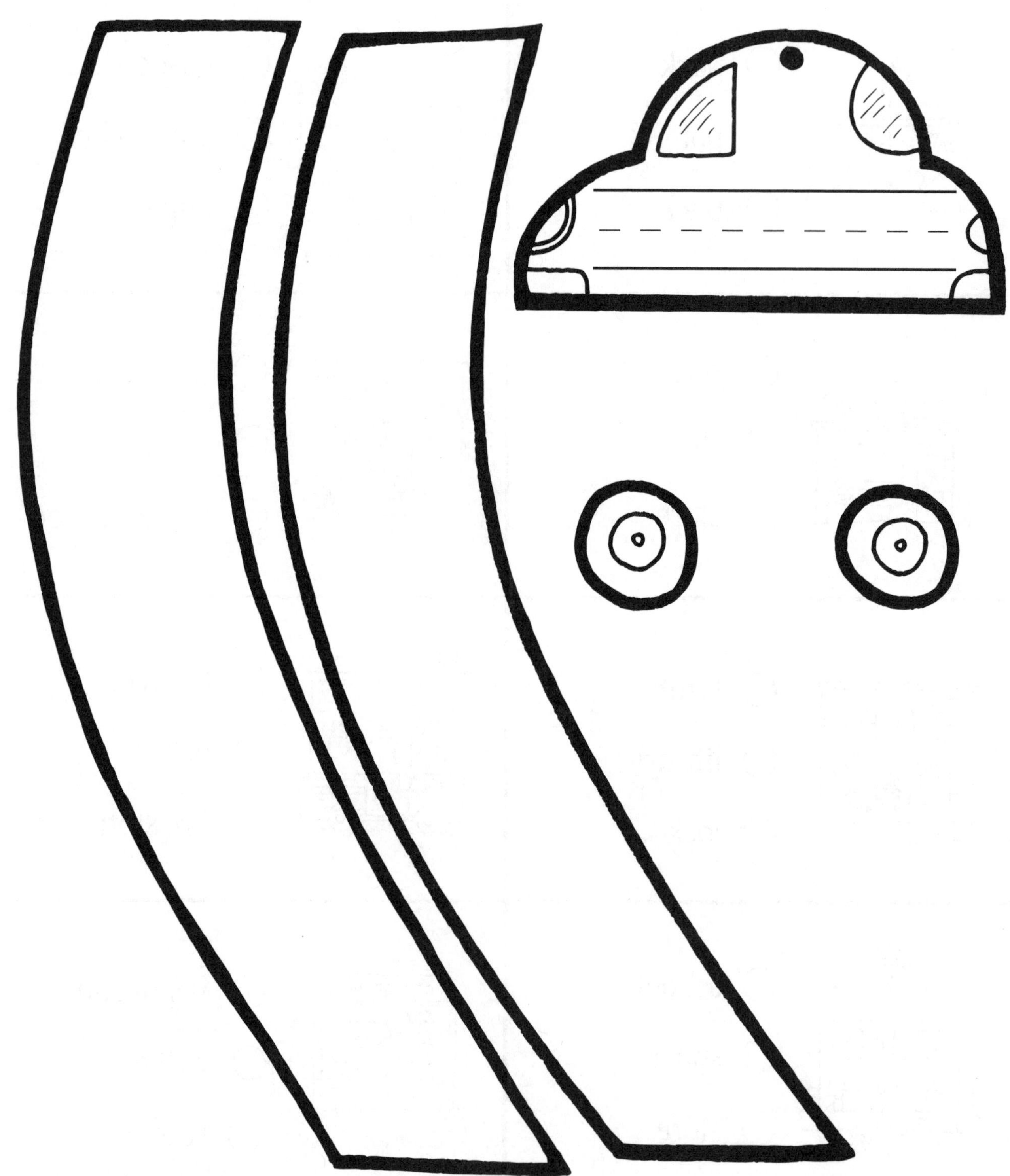

Buildings and Park Cutouts

Directions: Complete each sentence. Cut out the park and the buildings. Glue them to the inside of the file folder.

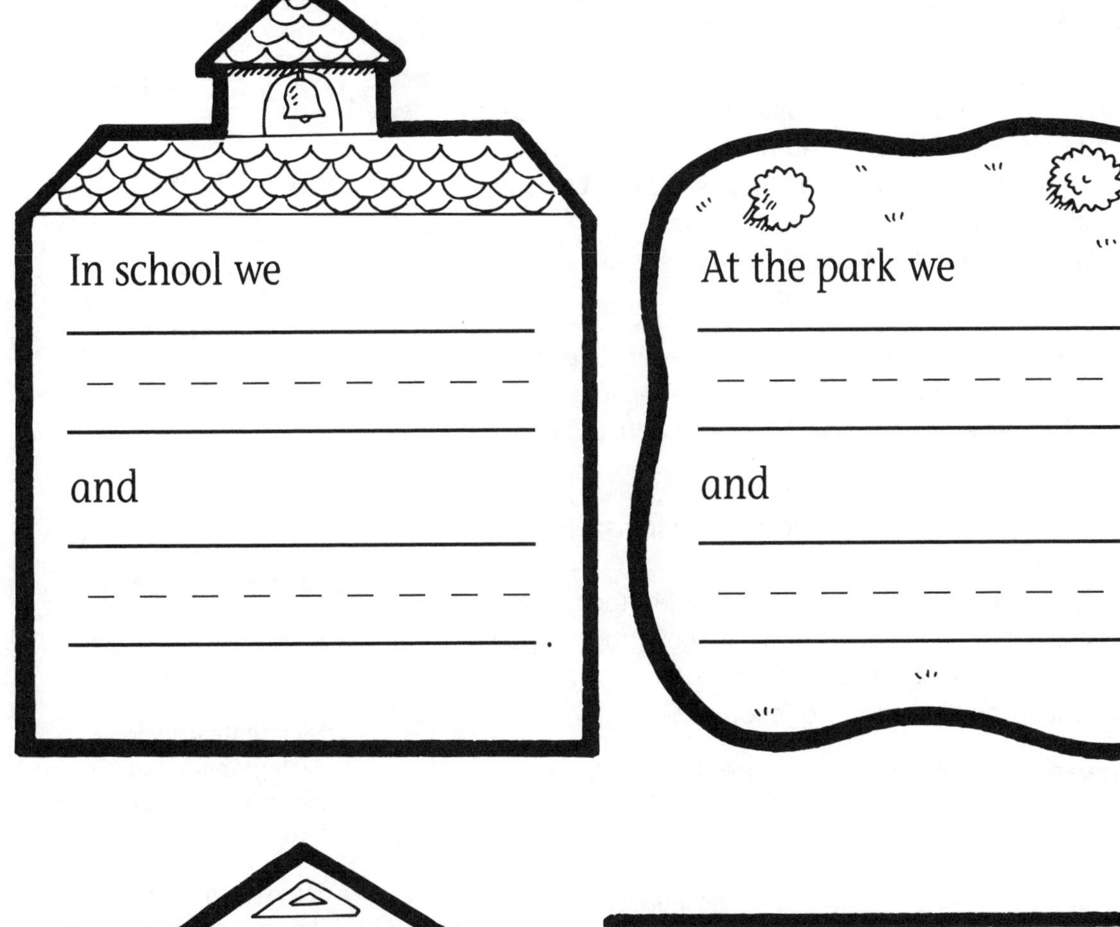

STORE

At the store we buy

and

LIBRARY

In the library we

and

Down Under

Preparation

Read aloud books about the ocean.

- *How to Hide an Octopus and Other Sea Creatures* by Ruth Heller (Econo-Clad Books)
- *The Magic School Bus on the Ocean Floor* by Joanna Cole (Scholastic)
- *Somewhere in the Ocean* by Jennifer Ward and T. J. Marsh (Rising Moon)

Gather a piece of blue construction paper for each student, two to four pieces of chart paper, and an X-ACTO® knife or razor blade (for teacher use only).

Make copies of these reproducibles.

- Ocean Word Recognition (page 111) transparency, class set of photocopies
- My Ocean Book (page 112) teacher photocopy and class set of photocopies on white construction paper
- Down Deep (page 113) transparency
- rubric (page 9) class set of photocopies

Prepare a sample My Ocean Book. (See Instructional Input.)

Setting the Stage

Ask if anyone has ever been on a boat or ship in the ocean. Talk about glass-bottom boats and submarines that allow people to look into the ocean. Invite students to arrange their chairs in the shape of a boat, close their eyes, and pretend they are on a boat looking deep into the water. Encourage them to use complete sentences to share what they are seeing. Record their responses on a piece of chart paper to make a word bank.

OBJECTIVE

The student will write sentences that tell about ocean animals.

CRITICAL COMPONENTS

- Sentences include facts about ocean animals.
- Each sentence and each proper noun begin with a capital letter.
- Each sentence ends with the correct punctuation.

Instructional Input

1 Give each student an Ocean Word Recognition reproducible. Invite volunteers to identify the picture in each box. Say several sentences using the word in the picture. For example, say *A crab lives in the ocean. I would like to eat a crab. I have a hermit crab in my fish tank.* Tell students to fill in the bubble next to the word that best describes the picture.

2 Display the Ocean Word Recognition overhead transparency. Review the correct answers, and have students circle them.

3 Show students the sample My Ocean Book you prepared. Give each student a My Ocean Book reproducible and art supplies.

4 Invite students to cut the My Ocean Book reproducible along the thick line and the dotted line to make a front cover for the book they will publish at the end of the lesson. Have them trace the waves cutout on blue construction paper and cut it out to make the back cover for the book. Invite them to write their name on the front cover and color it blue. Tell students to color each picture on the strip they cut off the bottom of the reproducible and write the correct word under each picture. As students are coloring, cutting, and writing, use an X-ACTO® knife or razor blade to carefully cut two slits in the front cover of each student's book. Demonstrate how to slide the strip through the slits. Collect the books to use in Guided Practice and Independent Practice.

Guided Practice

1 Display the Down Deep overhead transparency. Read aloud the paragraph with the blanks. Reread the paragraph, and invite students to help you fill in the blanks. Invite students to read aloud the completed paragraph along with you.

2 Give each student his or her My Ocean Book. Tell students which ocean animal to show on their front cover by moving the strip. Invite several volunteers to say a sentence about that ocean animal. Repeat this process until students have discussed all the animals and every student has had a turn to share a sentence. Record the sentences on several pieces of chart paper.

Independent Practice

1 Invite students to reread the facts about ocean animals you recorded on chart paper in Guided Practice. Encourage them to add more facts to the list.

2 Write on the board *A _____ has _______ and _____________.* Have students refer to their My Ocean Book. Tell students to choose at least four of the ocean animals on their strip. Have them write about each animal on a separate piece of paper. Encourage them to use the sentence frame to help them begin. For example, a student might write *A shark has large sharp teeth and a long gray body. It eats seals and fish. Sharks are fast swimmers.* Invite students to use the word bank and facts you recorded on chart paper.

3 Have students revise and edit their rough drafts and then use the rubric to evaluate their writing.

Presentation

- Have students **publish** their final drafts on sheets of white lined paper and staple them into their My Ocean Book.
- Encourage students to **share** their completed books with partners or in small groups.

TEACHING HINTS/EXTENSIONS

- Tell students that the largest whale is the blue whale and it measures 102 feet (31.11 m) in length. On a large cement or blacktop surface, invite students to use a measuring tape or several yardsticks and chalk to mark 102 feet. Ask half the class to stand at the nose and half at the tail so that they can appreciate how enormous the whale is. Measure students to see how tall they are, and have them mark their heights on the ground next to the blue whale's measurement. Ask students to compare the whale's length with their heights.
- Divide the class into small groups. Write the letters of the words *atlantic ocean* on separate index cards for each group. (Do not capitalize any letters because it will confuse students and make them think they have to begin words with the capitalized letters only.) Challenge each group to use the letters to make as many words (e.g., lane, tie, net) as they can in 15 minutes. Have students record the words on paper and share them with the class.

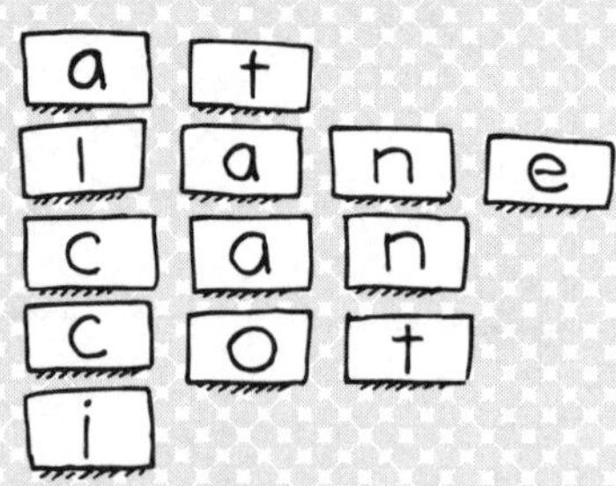

- Teach a unit about whales. An entire unit on whales is available on-line from the College of Library and Information Science, University of South Carolina Web site at www.libsci.sc.edu/miller/whales.htm. This site contains many whale activities, Internet resources, video recommendations, and an extensive literature list of both fiction and nonfiction books.
- Have students complete one or more of these writing prompts in a journal:
  - ✔ Write about the animals in the ocean.
  - ✔ Write about the plants in the ocean.
  - ✔ Write about how the ocean is different from land.

Name ______________________________ Date ______________________

Ocean Word Recognition

Directions: Fill in the bubble next to the word that best describes the picture.

○ eat
○ eel
○ ear

○ open
○ oar
○ ocean

○ sand
○ sat
○ sardine

○ wet
○ what
○ whale

○ fish
○ feet
○ fire

○ crab
○ crack
○ can

○ shop
○ shark
○ sand

○ rain
○ ray
○ race

My Ocean Book

Directions: Cut along the thick line. Cut along the dotted line to remove the strip of ocean animals. Trace the shape on blue construction paper and cut it out to make a back cover. Write your name on the front cover and color it blue. Color the animals and write their names on the strip. Slide the strip through the slits cut by your teacher.

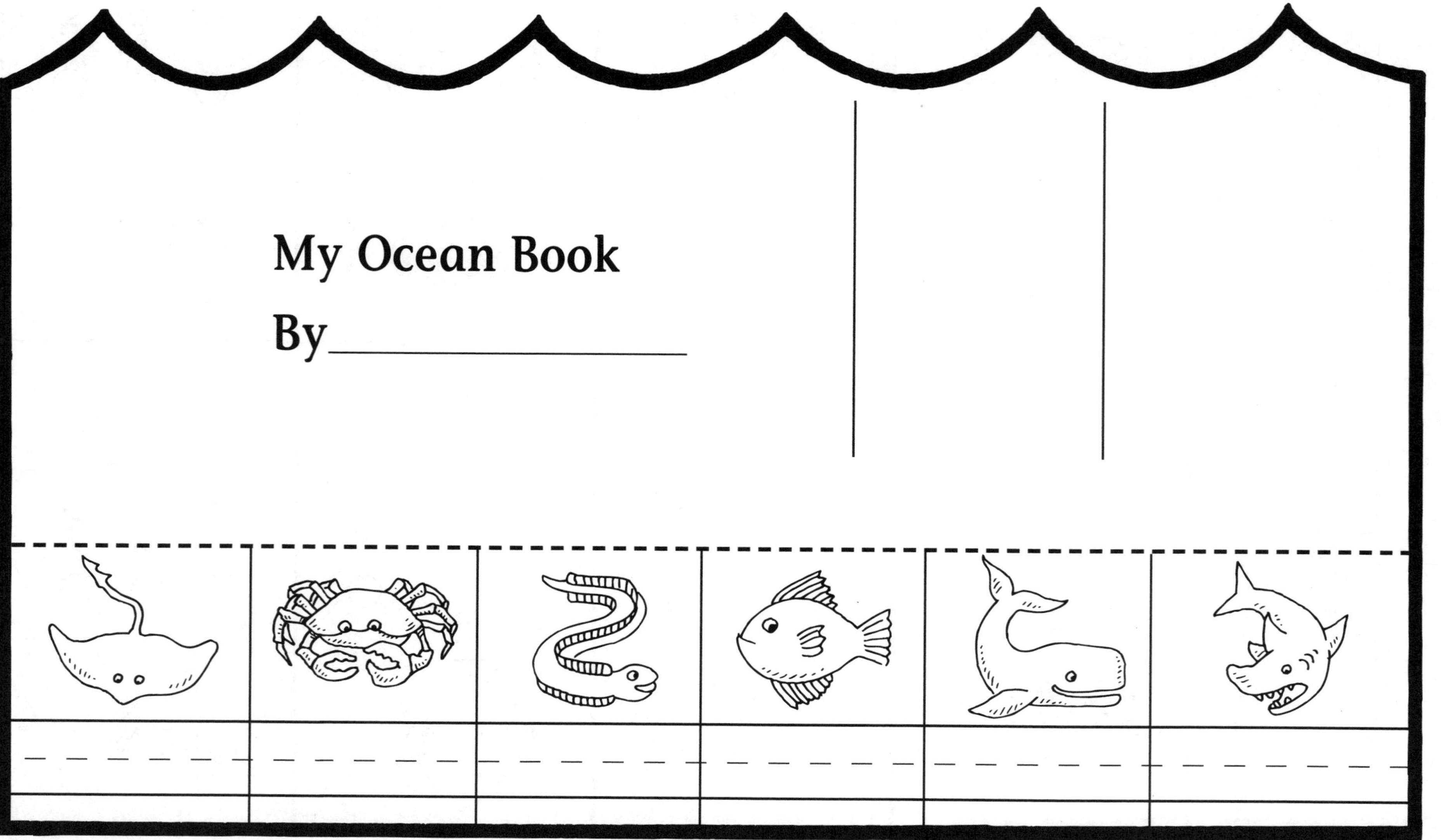

Down Deep

Directions: Fill in the blanks with a word from the parentheses.

The ______________________ is home to many animals.
(ocean, whale, sharks)

The largest animal is the blue ______________________.
(fish, whale, sand)

Not only ______________________ live in the ocean, but
(sand, fish, ocean)

______________________ and rays do, too. Along the
(sharks, sand, ocean)

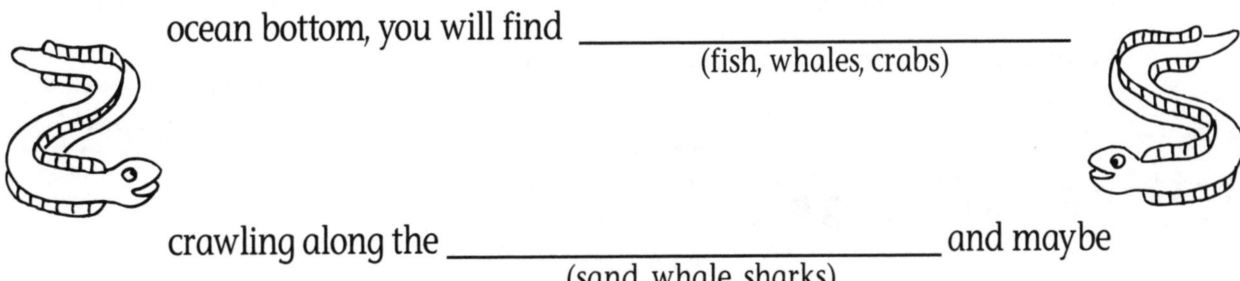

ocean bottom, you will find ______________________
(fish, whales, crabs)

crawling along the ______________________ and maybe
(sand, whale, sharks)

an ______________________ hiding behind a rock.
(fish, eel, whale)

Back to Nature

Preparation

Read aloud books about the forest.

- *Forest (An I Can Read Book)* by Laura Godwin (HarperCollins)
- *Forest Life* by Barbara Taylor (DK Publishing)
- *In Woods & Forests* by Tessa Paul (Crabtree Publishing)

Gather a class set of clipboards with blank paper and pencils, two brass fasteners for the teacher and each student, and two pieces of chart paper.

Make copies of these reproducibles.

- Forest Word Recognition (page 117) transparency, class set of photocopies
- In the Forest (page 118) transparency, class set of photocopies
- Deer Head Pattern (page 119) two teacher photocopies and two class sets of photocopies on brown construction paper
- Visit to the Wooded Forest (page 120) transparency, class set of photocopies
- rubric (page 9) class set of photocopies

Prepare a sample Deer Shape Book. (See Guided Practice.)

Setting the Stage

Take students to a park or an area with trees. Give each student a clipboard, paper, and a pencil. Ask students to close their eyes and concentrate on what they hear. Have them record what they heard on the paper. Have them look around without speaking. Invite them to sketch pictures of several things they see. Return to the classroom, and encourage students to share what they heard and saw. Then, ask students to share any experiences they have had walking in a forest or what they would see if they did visit a forest. As students share and brainstorm ideas, record their responses on a piece of chart paper to make a word bank about the forest.

OBJECTIVE

The student will write sentences that tell about the forest.

CRITICAL COMPONENTS

- Sentences include facts about the forest.
- Each sentence and each proper noun begin with a capital letter.
- Each sentence ends with the correct punctuation.

Instructional Input

1 Give each student a Forest Word Recognition reproducible. Invite volunteers to identify the plant or animal in each box. Say several sentences about each plant or animal. For example, say *A rabbit is white. A rabbit lives in the forest. I have a pet rabbit.* Tell students to fill in the bubble next to the name of the plant or animal.

2 Display the Forest Word Recognition overhead transparency. Review the correct answers, and have students circle them.

3 Give each student an In the Forest reproducible, and display the overhead transparency. Read aloud the story, and then invite the class to read it aloud with you. Encourage students to act out the story, including sound effects, as you slowly read it a third time.

4 Encourage students to reread the story on their own and underline the animals in it. Tell them to fill in the bubbles next to the animals that were in the forest in the story (i.e., birds, rabbits, squirrel, frog, deer). Record the correct answers on the transparency. Ask students if any other animals were in the story. Have students write these animals (i.e., insects, cougar) below the list. Ask if the other animals that remain on the list could be found in a forest, and discuss where they live.

5 Have students name all the animals that can be found in a forest. Record their responses on a piece of chart paper to make a word bank.

Guided Practice

1 Lead a discussion about deer. Ask students where deer live, what they eat, and how they behave. Talk about deer body parts and how they help them survive in the forest (e.g., ears help them hear predators, nose helps them smell danger).

2 Give each student two Deer Head Pattern reproducibles and two brass fasteners. Show the sample Deer Shape Book you prepared.

3 Tell students to cut out each deer head and ear. Invite them to draw two eyes, a nose, and a mouth on one of the heads.

4 Tell students to staple the two heads together at the top and attach the ears to the back head with brass fasteners. Have students write a title and their name on the front head. (These heads will be used to create individual books.)

Independent Practice

1 Display the word banks you recorded in Setting the Stage and Instructional Input. Invite volunteers to read aloud the information.

2 Display the Visit to the Wooded Forest overhead transparency. Have students copy the sentence frames on separate pieces of lined paper. Have them write about the forest by completing the sentences. For example, a student might write *If I took a walk in the forest, I might see rabbits hopping and squirrels scampering.*

3 Have students revise and edit their rough draft and then use the rubric to evaluate their writing.

Presentation

- Have students **publish** their final drafts on the Visit to the Wooded Forest reproducibles and cut their sentences apart. Have students write additional sentences on white lined paper cut to be the same size as the reproducibles. Have students staple these sheets to the inside of their back deer head to make individual books.
- Encourage students to **share** their books with partners or in small groups.
- **Display** the shape books on a bulletin board decorated as a forest.

TEACHING HINTS/EXTENSIONS

- Talk about the food chain. For example, say *The leaves are eaten by a caterpillar, a praying mantis eats the caterpillar, and an owl eats the praying mantis.* Write *leaves, caterpillar, praying mantis,* and *owl* on separate index cards. Invite volunteers to each hold up a card. Ask the class to put the cards in the correct order to demonstrate the food chain. Repeat the activity with other examples, such as fly, frog, snake, hawk; or acorns, squirrel, coyote.
- Read aloud a book about Daniel Boone. Discuss his life (1734–1829) and his role in the history of our country. Ask students to tell what the forest was like during the time that Daniel Boone lived. Invite them to talk about hunting for food in the forest instead of grocery shopping. Invite students to write several sentences about Daniel Boone.
- Read aloud *Frog, Where Are You?* by Mercer Mayer (Dial Books). Invite students to think of a new adventure for the frog. Encourage them to write several sentences about this new adventure.
- Have students complete one or more of these writing prompts in a journal:
  - ✔ Imagine you were walking in the forest and found a hurt animal. Write about how you took care of it.
  - ✔ Pretend to climb a tree in the forest and write about what you see.
  - ✔ Write about why it is important to take care of the forest.

Name ______________________________ Date ____________________

Forest Word Recognition

Directions: Fill in the bubble next to the name of the plant or animal.

○ bird
○ bag
○ bite

○ plant
○ pot
○ play

○ three
○ tree
○ trip

○ inside
○ insect
○ icicle

○ flour
○ float
○ flower

○ deer
○ drop
○ dear

○ rat
○ rabbit
○ racket

○ base
○ bear
○ bake

Name ______________________ Date ______________________

In the Forest

It was early morning in the forest. A cool breeze made a rustling sound as it passed through the lush green trees. A deer was nibbling on some grass in a clearing. Several insects were crawling on the ground beneath the dried leaves and twigs. As the water from a stream splashed against the rocks, a frog made croaking noises. Birds could be heard chirping and calling to each other. Several rabbits hopped among the green plants looking for something to eat. A chattering squirrel jumped down from a log and scampered away. Suddenly, the deer turned its ears and lifted its head to look around. Its nose twitched as it sniffed the breeze. A twig snapped. The deer turned and quickly ran into the forest. As it disappeared into the trees, a cougar stepped into the clearing, stared at the departing deer, and slowly walked away.

Directions: Fill in the bubbles next to the animals that were in the forest in the story.

○ bear
○ birds
○ rabbits
○ skunk
○ owl

○ squirrel
○ frog
○ beaver
○ deer
○ snake

Deer Head Pattern

Directions: Cut out two heads and two ears. Draw two eyes, a nose, and a mouth on one of the heads. Staple the two heads together at the top. Attach the ears to the back head with brass fasteners. Write a title and your name on the front head.

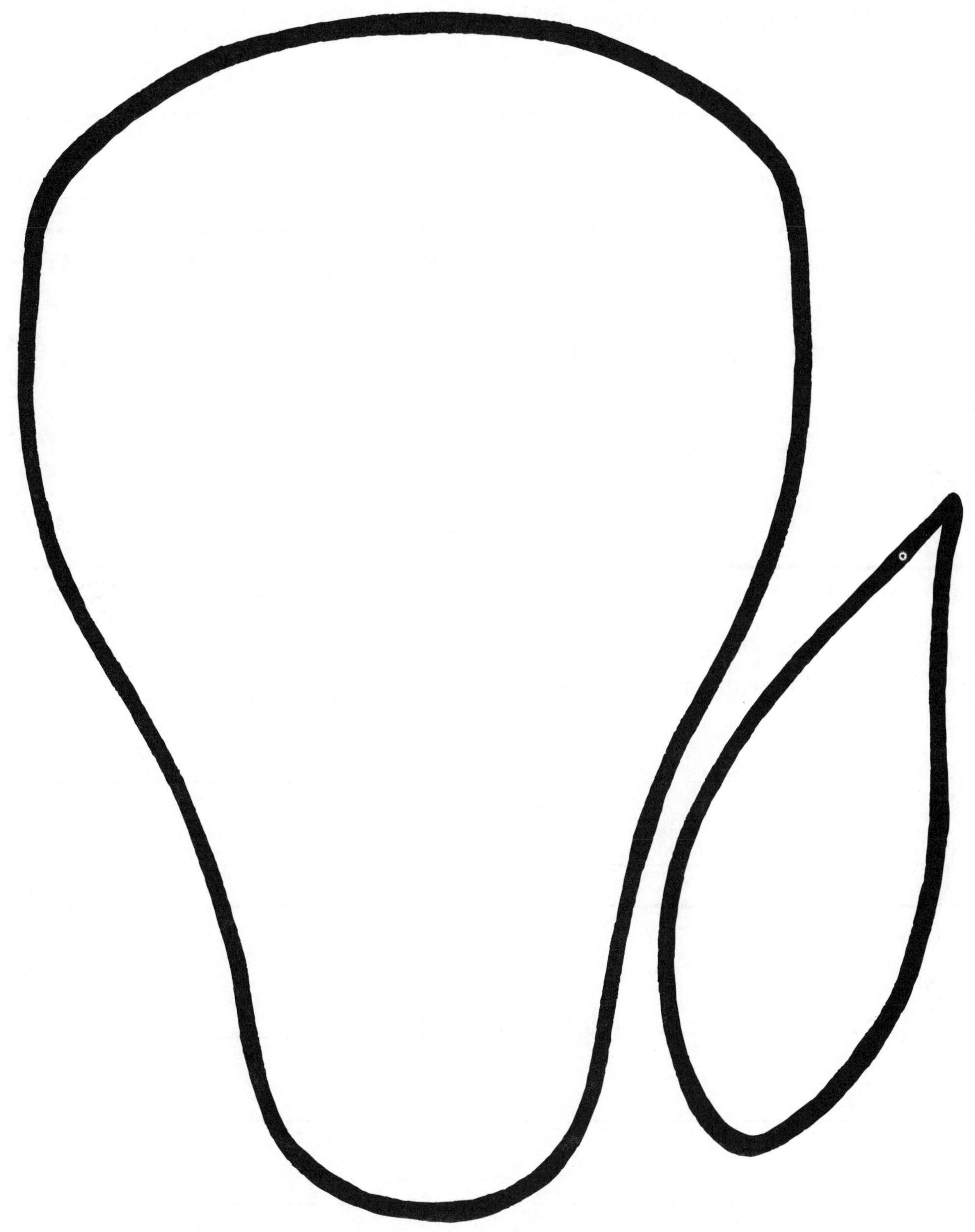

Visit to the Wooded Forest

If I take a walk in the forest, I might see ______________________

____

and ____ .

If I am very quiet, I might hear ______________________

____

and ____ .

If I look closely at the ground, I might see ______________________

____

and ____ .

If I am not careful, I might discover a ______________________

____

or a ____ .

E-I-E-I-O

Preparation

Read aloud books about farms.

- *Farm Animals* by Gallimard Jeunesse (Cartwheel Books®)
- *Farmer Brown Goes Round and Round* by Teri Sloat (DK Publishing)
- *My First Visit to the Farm* by Jose M. Parramon (Barron's)

Gather two pieces of chart paper, a pocket chart, and index cards.

Make copies of these reproducibles.

- Animal Cards (page 124) teacher photocopy and one photocopy on card stock for each pair of students
- Farm Word Recognition (page 125) transparency, class set of photocopies
- Barn Shape Book (page 126) class set of photocopies
- rubric (page 9) class set of photocopies

Setting the Stage

Divide the class into groups of two. Give each pair of students an Animal Cards reproducible. Ask students to cut apart the cards and sort them into groups. Encourage students to use any attribute they may think of (e.g., have fur, live on land, live in water, found at the zoo) to group the animals. Ask pairs of students to share and explain the groups they made.

OBJECTIVE

The student will write sentences that tell about farm animals.

CRITICAL COMPONENTS

- Sentences include facts about farm animals.
- Each sentence and each proper noun begin with a capital letter.
- Each sentence ends with the correct punctuation.

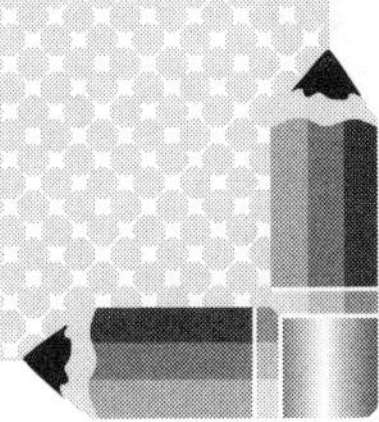

Instructional Input

1 Display a set of animal cards in a pocket chart. Ask students to identify which animals would be part of a group of farm animals. If students leave out any of the farm animals, add those cards to the group.

2 Ask students what other animals might be found on a farm, write each one on an index card, and add these cards to the pocket chart to make a word bank.

3 Discuss the reasons that farm animals are important. Record on a piece of chart paper the food we get from farm animals, the products we get from them, and the work they do for humans. For example, you might write *A cow gives milk. A sheep provides wool. Dogs herd animals.*

Guided Practice

1 Give each student a Farm Word Recognition reproducible. Invite volunteers to identify the picture in each box. Say several sentences about each picture. For example, say *A pig is pink. I like the curly tail on the back of a pig. I saw a pig at the farm.* Tell students to fill in the bubble next to the word that best describes the picture.

2 Display the Farm Word Recognition overhead transparency. Review the correct answers, and have students circle them.

3 Write on the board, a blank transparency, or sentence strips *We get ____ from a ______. A _______ helps the farmer _______.*

4 Invite students to orally complete the sentences to tell facts about farm animals (e.g., *We get pork from a pig. A cat helps the farmer catch mice*). Record their responses on a piece of chart paper.

5 Invite students to draw a farm scene and write at least one sentence about what the animals in the picture give to or do for the farmer. Collect the pages, and staple them together to make a class book.

Independent Practice

1 Have students write several sentences about farm animals. Tell them to write about which animals live on a farm, what food and products they give to farmers, or the work they do. If students need help with ideas or vocabulary, encourage them to refer to the pocket chart word bank or the list you recorded in Instructional Input.

2 Have students revise and edit their rough draft and then use the rubric to evaluate their writing.

Presentation

- Have students **publish** their final drafts on the Barn Shape Book reproducibles. (If students need more writing lines, photocopy additional pages, or have students trace the barn shape on lined paper.)
- Have students **create** front and back covers for their shape book by cutting out the barn shape, tracing it on construction paper, cutting out their tracings, and writing a title and author.
- **Make** individual books by laminating each cover, hole-punching the covers and pages, and tieing the pages together with yarn.
- **Display** the shape books in the classroom library.

TEACHING HINTS/EXTENSIONS

- Invite students to dress up as their farm animals and read their books to a class of younger students.

- Have students create a mural or a collage of a farm on the classroom wall. Invite them to add animals and other scenery that belongs on a farm.
- Color and cut apart a set of animal cards. Create another set of cards that illustrate and name what each animal gives us or what it does on the farm. Have students shuffle the cards and lay them out facedown in rows. Invite students to take turns turning over two cards at a time and reading them aloud. If the cards match (e.g., cow—milk or dog—herd sheep), have the student keep the pair and take another turn. If the cards do not match, have the player turn them facedown again, and invite the next player to take a turn. Have students continue to play until they have matched all the cards.
- Have students complete one or more of these writing prompts in a journal:
  - ✔ Imagine you are writing to someone who has never been on a farm. How would you describe it to this person?
  - ✔ If you could be a farm animal, which animal would you be? Why?
  - ✔ Write about the crops a farmer might grow.

Animal Cards

Name ______________________________ Date ______________________________

Farm Word Recognition

Directions: Fill in the bubble next to the word that best describes the picture.

- ○ coat
- ○ cow
- ○ cap

- ○ pie
- ○ pin
- ○ pig

- ○ chicken
- ○ cheese
- ○ can

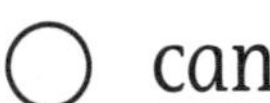

- ○ go
- ○ gopher
- ○ goat

- ○ wood
- ○ work
- ○ wool

- ○ chase
- ○ cheese
- ○ chop

- ○ wood
- ○ wool
- ○ water

- ○ mint
- ○ milk
- ○ mice

Barn Shape Book

Green, Green Everywhere

Preparation

Read aloud books about the rain forest.

- *About the Rain Forest (We Both Read Series)* by Heather Johanasen (Treasure Bay)
- *The Great Kapok Tree: A Tale of the Amazon Rain Forest* by Lynne Cherry (Voyager)
- *Where the Forest Meets the Sea* by Jeannie Baker (William Morrow & Company)

Gather nonfiction books about the rain forest for the classroom library and four pieces of chart paper.

Obtain the video *The Magic School Bus in the Rainforest: A Tropical Paradise Adventure* (Scholastic). Arrange to have a television and VCR in the classroom.

Make copies of these reproducibles.

- Rain Forest Word Recognition (page 130) transparency, class set of photocopies
- My Mini Rain Forest Book (page 131) transparency, class set of photocopies
- writing template (page 132) class set of photocopies
- rubric (page 9) class set of photocopies

Setting the Stage

Ask students if they have ever seen a forest (in real life, in a book, on TV). Invite them to share what kinds of animals and plants live there. Record their responses on a piece of chart paper. Discuss why the forest is important, and record their responses. Tell students that they are going to be learning about a special kind of forest called a rain forest. Ask them to share what they think a rain forest might be like. Ask students to predict which of the animals and plants on the brainstormed list might be found in a rain forest. Circle or underline the animals and plants they name.

Forest

trees	squirrels
bushes	birds
oak trees	rabbits
pine trees	snakes
berry bushes	insects
	spiders

OBJECTIVE

The student will write sentences that tell about the rain forest.

CRITICAL COMPONENTS

- Sentences include facts about the rain forest.
- Each sentence and each proper noun begin with a capital letter.
- Each sentence ends with the correct punctuation.

Instructional Input

1 Share one or two nonfiction rain forest books with the class. Point out the plants and animals found in the rain forest and also the importance of the rain forest.

2 Ask students to check their predictions of which animals and plants live in the rain forest that you circled or underlined on the list you recorded in Setting the Stage.

3 Have students brainstorm word banks for rain forest animals, rain forest plants, and the importance of the rain forest. Record their responses on separate pieces of chart paper.

4 Give each student a Rain Forest Word Recognition reproducible. Invite volunteers to identify the picture in each box. Say several sentences about the picture. For example, say *A parrot is a bird. A parrot has colorful feathers. I have seen a parrot in a tree.* Tell students to fill in the bubble next to the word that best describes the picture.

5 Display the Rain Forest Word Recognition overhead transparency. Review the correct answers, and have students circle them.

Guided Practice

1 Show the video *The Magic School Bus in the Rainforest: A Tropical Paradise Adventure.* Discuss the animals and plants students saw in the video and what they learned about the rain forest. Add any new information to the word banks you recorded in Instructional Input.

2 Give each student a My Mini Rain Forest Book reproducible, and display the overhead transparency. Read aloud the sentence frames. Reread them, and say the words listed below the blanks. Have students complete the sentences with the words provided or their own words. Encourage them to use the list from Setting the Stage and the word banks from Instructional Input. Ask students to illustrate their sentences, cut apart the pages, and staple the book together.

3 Encourage students to read their sentences and show their illustrations to the class.

Independent Practice

1 Invite students to write several factual sentences about the rain forest. Tell students they can write about the animals or plants that live in the rain forest, about why the rain forest is important, or about protecting the rain forest. Encourage them to use the word banks and information you recorded throughout the lesson if they need ideas or vocabulary.

2 Have students revise and edit their rough draft and then use the rubric to evaluate their writing.

Presentation

- Have students **publish** their final drafts and illustrations on the writing templates. (If students need more writing lines, photocopy additional pages.)
- **Display** students' writing on a bulletin board decorated like a rain forest.
- Encourage students to **share** their writing with classmates in a "Round the Room" format, in which they take turns standing at their seats and reading aloud their writing.

TEACHING HINTS/EXTENSIONS

- Explain the layers of the rain forest (i.e., emergent layer, canopy, understory, forest floor) to students. Invite students to help you create a word bank for the animals found in each layer. Post the word banks in a writing center where students can write about the animals found in each layer of the rain forest or create a mural to illustrate the layers and the animals that live in them.
- Discuss the importance of rain forests and the dangers they are facing. Have students create "Save the Rain Forest" posters. Display them throughout the school.
- Challenge students to create math story problems that include alliteration to describe rain forest animals. For example, a student might write *Six slow sloths met two talking toucans. How many animals were there?* (6 sloths + 2 toucans = 8 animals) Have students write these stories individually, with a partner, or in a group. Have students illustrate their story problems, and combine them into a class book.

- Have students complete one or more of these writing prompts in a journal:
  - ✔ You are in the rain forest. What do you see?
  - ✔ You are in the rain forest. What do you hear?
  - ✔ You are in the rain forest. Why is this place special? Why should we be careful to preserve the rain forest?

Name ______________________________ Date ____________________

Rain Forest Word Recognition

Directions: Fill in the bubble next to the word that best describes the picture.

○ kite
○ Kapok Tree
○ cactus

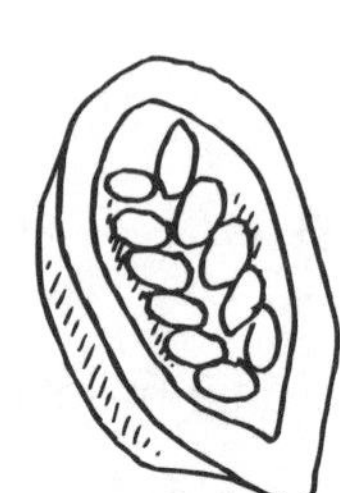

○ captain
○ cake
○ cacao beans

○ pat
○ patio
○ parrot

○ frog
○ fern
○ frame

○ juggler
○ jaguar
○ jar

○ happy
○ horse
○ home

○ air plant
○ airplane
○ actor

○ slot
○ snake
○ sloth

My Mini Rain Forest Book

By

____

____________________ live in the
(Snakes, Dogs, Cows)

rain forest.

____________________ grow in the
(Cacti, Tomatoes, Ferns)

rain forest.

The rain forest is important because it gives us

____________________.
(heat, oxygen, milk)

Name ______________________ Date ______________________

It's Cold

Preparation

Read aloud books about the arctic tundra.

- *Arctic Tundra: Land with No Trees* by Allan Fowler (Grolier Publishing)
- *One Small Square: Arctic Tundra* by Donald M. Silver (McGraw-Hill)
- *Polar Mammals (A True Book)* by Larry Dane Brimner (Children's Press)

Gather nonfiction books about the arctic tundra for use in the classroom library, two pieces of chart paper, yarn or a metal ring, and a class set of sentence strips.

Obtain a globe or a map that shows the location of the arctic tundra.

Make copies of these reproducibles.
- Web (page 136) transparency, class set of photocopies
- Arctic Word Recognition (page 137) transparency, class set of photocopies
- Igloo Shape Book (page 138) class set of photocopies
- rubric (page 9) class set of photocopies

Setting the Stage

Show students a map or a globe, and point out the Arctic Circle. Explain that this is the northernmost part of the earth and the land and animals there are unique in many ways. Continue to explain that the winters there are very cold and dark. Say *During winter, the sun does not shine on that part of the earth. During summer, the sun never sets on that part of the earth, but it still does not get very warm. Only the surface snow and ice melt; the ground underneath (the permafrost) stays frozen.* Ask students what they think it is like in a place like that, what animals might live there, and what plants might grow there. Record their responses on a piece of chart paper.

OBJECTIVE

The student will write sentences that tell about the arctic tundra.

CRITICAL COMPONENTS

- Sentences include facts about the arctic tundra.
- Each sentence and each proper noun begin with a capital letter.
- Each sentence ends with the correct punctuation.

Instructional Input

1 Share with the class one or two nonfiction books about the arctic tundra. Point out the plants and animals that live there and what the environment is like. Record the plants, the animals, and information about the environment on a piece of chart paper.

2 Give each student a Web reproducible, and display the overhead transparency. Invite students to help you create a web that describes the arctic tundra and record the information on their reproducible. (You may want to make your web on a large piece of butcher paper so that it can be saved and posted on the classroom wall.) Use the example below as a guide.

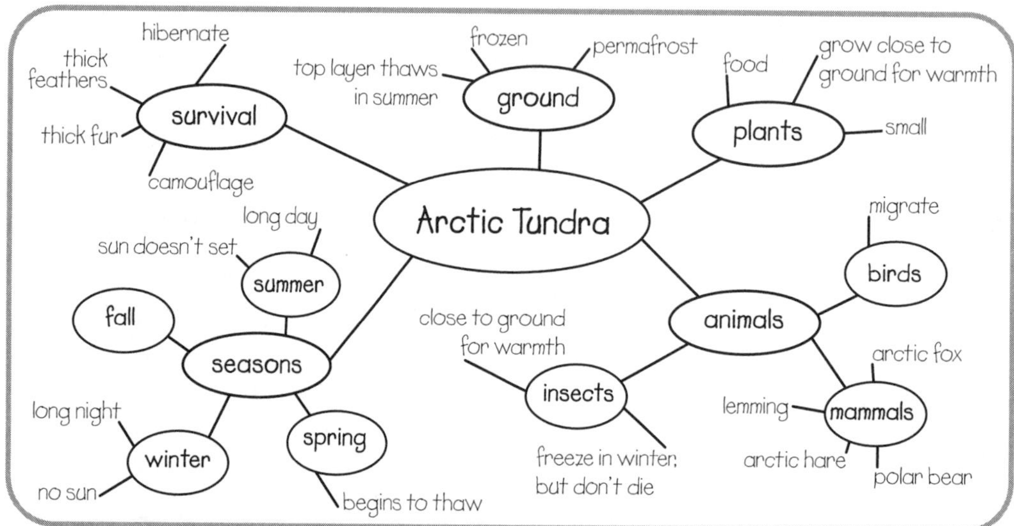

3 Have students compare the information recorded on the web with the predictions they made during Setting the Stage. Discuss whether or not their predictions were correct. Talk about the things that they learned that are different from what they predicted.

Guided Practice

1 Give each student an Arctic Word Recognition reproducible. Invite volunteers to identify the picture in each box. Say several sentences about each picture. For example, say *A bear will hibernate every winter. A bear will hibernate when it is cold. Do people hibernate?* Tell students to fill in the bubble next to the word that best describes the picture.

2 Display the Arctic Word Recognition overhead transparency. Review the correct answers, and have students circle them.

3 Write on the board or on sentence strips *The _____ in the arctic tundra* __________. Model how to complete the sentence with facts from the class web and the list of predictions. For example, write *The ground in the arctic tundra is frozen* or *The plants in the arctic tundra grow close to the ground for heat*.

4 Invite students to give more examples of how to complete the sentence. Give each student a sentence strip, and have students write a sentence about the arctic tundra on it. Hole-punch the sentence strips, and connect them with yarn or a metal ring.

Independent Practice

1 Invite students to write several sentences that include facts about the arctic tundra. Tell them that they can write about the animals or plants that live there or what the environment is like. If students need help with ideas or vocabulary, encourage them to refer to the class web and the list you recorded in Instructional Input.

2 Have students revise and edit their rough draft and then use the rubric to evaluate their writing.

Presentation

- Have students **publish** their final drafts on the Igloo Shape Book reproducibles. (If students need more writing lines, photocopy additional pages, or have students trace the igloo shape on lined paper.)
- Have students **create** front and back covers for their shape book by cutting out the igloo shape, tracing it on construction paper, cutting out their tracings, and writing a title and their name on the front cover. Then, have them staple all their pages together to make individual books.
- Encourage students to **share** their books with the class or in small groups.
- **Display** student work on a bulletin board with a border of arctic animals.

TEACHING HINTS/EXTENSIONS

- Have students choose one arctic animal to learn more about. After students research their animal (with the help of parent volunteers or cross-age volunteers), have them write about the animal. If you do not have volunteers available to help you, have the class choose two or three animals to research together. After reading about the animals with the class, work together to chart the important information about each animal. Then, have students choose one of the animals to write about and use the charted information as a reference.
- Invite the class to create a mural to show what the arctic tundra looks like during the summer. Show the layers of thawed ground and permafrost. Include animals and plants. Have students label the animals on the mural.

- Invite students to make "igloos" outside on a cold day. Give students ice cubes and vanilla icing to connect them. Challenge students to make the largest igloo or the most unique looking igloo.
- Have students complete one or more of these writing prompts in a journal:
  - ✔ A scientist is moving to the arctic tundra for 12 months. What should he or she pack?
  - ✔ Describe the animals of the arctic. Tell what they look like, where they live, and what they eat.
  - ✔ What are igloos? How do people make them?

Name ______________________ Date ______________________

Web

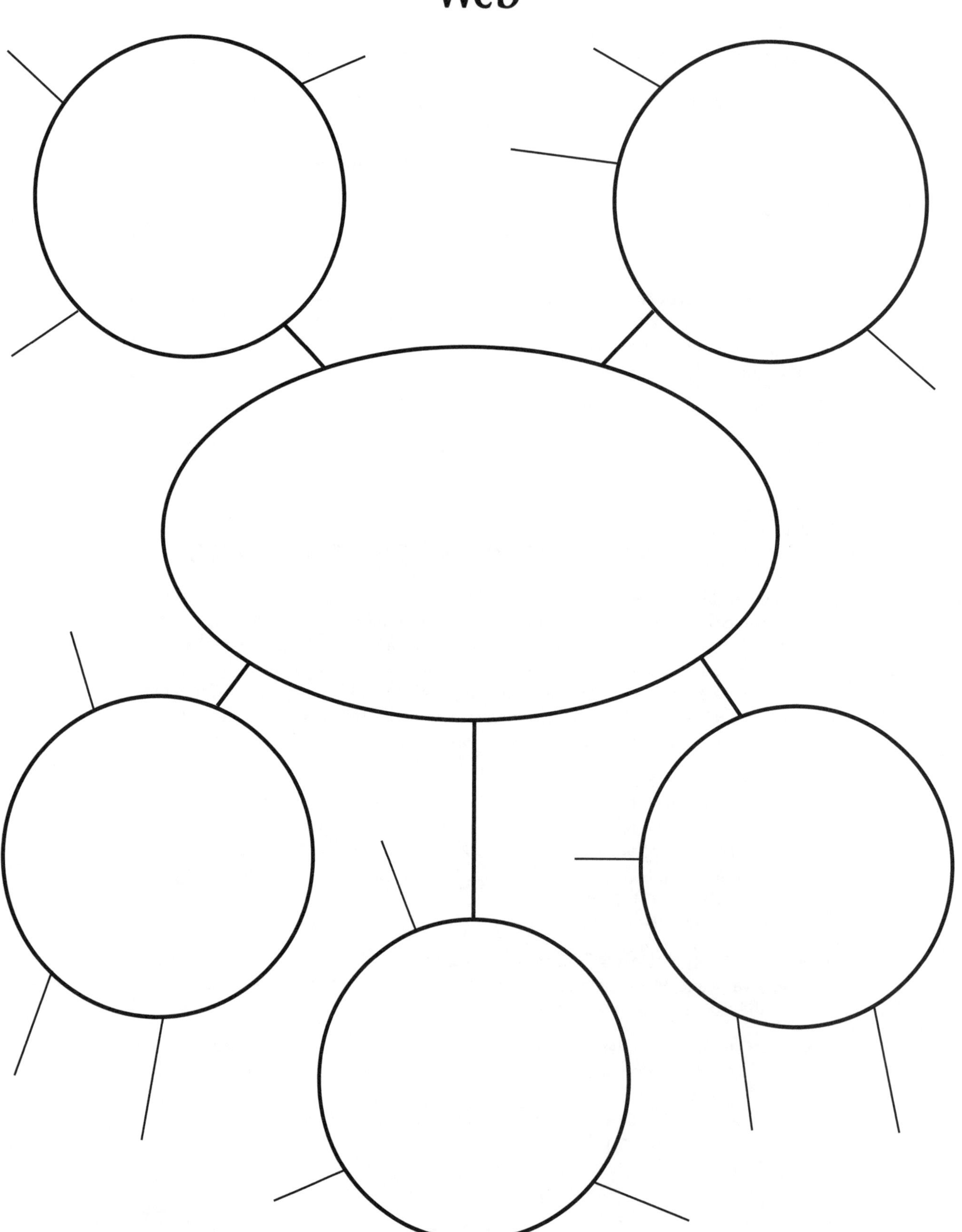

Name ______________________________ Date ______________________

Arctic Word Recognition

Directions: Fill in the bubble next to the word that best describes the picture.

- ○ hare
- ○ hair
- ○ hard

- ○ fur
- ○ feathers
- ○ fed

- ○ permafrost
- ○ park
- ○ port

- ○ burns
- ○ birds
- ○ bite

- ○ water
- ○ winter
- ○ wind

- ○ ton
- ○ tug
- ○ tundra

- ○ hibernate
- ○ hide
- ○ higher

- ○ maps
- ○ mammals
- ○ magic

Igloo Shape Book

All-Stars

Preparation

Read aloud books about sports.

- *Ronald Morgan Goes to Bat* by Patricia Reilly Giff (Viking)
- *Soccer Sam* by Jean Marzollo (Random House Books)
- *Sports! Sports! Sports!: A Poetry Collection (An I Can Read Book)* by Lee Bennett Hopkins (HarperCollins)

Invite guests (e.g., P. E. teacher, parents, local sports figure) to your classroom to talk about their favorite sport and show the equipment they use and pictures of the sport.

Gather two pieces of chart paper and two blank overhead transparencies.

Create flash cards for the words *baseball, football, basketball, volleyball, tennis, swimming, soccer,* and *skiing.*

Make copies of these reproducibles.

- Sports Word Recognition (page 142) transparency, class set of photocopies
- All-Star Sports (page 143) transparency, class set of photocopies
- My Favorite Sports (page 144) transparency, class set of photocopies
- rubric (page 9) class set of photocopies

Setting the Stage

Have guests visit your classroom and discuss their favorite sport. Ask them to share some of the equipment they use and pictures or videotapes of themselves in action. Have students share what their favorite sport is and why. Encourage students to draw a picture to illustrate why they like the sport. Invite them to brainstorm a list of sports. Record their responses on a piece of chart paper to make a word bank. Remind students that sports don't only include the ones played by professional athletes. They also include games played at school or home.

OBJECTIVE

The student will write several sentences about his or her favorite sports.

CRITICAL COMPONENTS

- Sentences identify two favorite sports.
- Sentences include details about why the student likes the sports.
- Sentences tell how the sports are played and what equipment is needed.
- Each sentence and each proper noun begin with a capital letter.
- Each sentence ends with the correct punctuation.

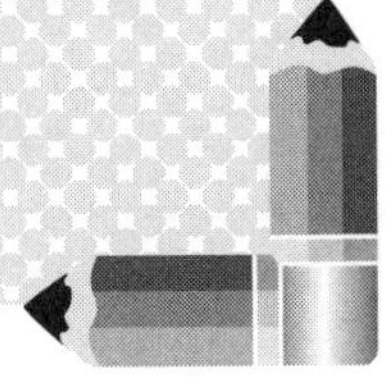

Instructional Input

1 Show students the sports flash cards, and read aloud each word. Review the words by having students read them chorally as you show each word.

2 Tape the flash cards on the board or a wall, or place them in a pocket chart. Have students explain what equipment is needed for each sport and what types of activities take place during that sport. Record their responses on a piece of chart paper.

3 Divide the class into eight groups. Give each group a flash card. Ask groups to silently read the word and then briefly pantomime participating in this sport. Invite the class to identify each sport.

4 Give each student a Sports Word Recognition reproducible. Invite volunteers to identify what sport is played with the equipment in each box. Say several sentences about each sport. For example, say *I like to bounce a tennis ball. Do you know how to play tennis? Tennis is a sport.* Tell students to fill in the bubble next to the name of the sport.

5 Display the Sports Word Recognition overhead transparency. Review the correct answers, and have students circle them.

Guided Practice

1 Read aloud the words on the sports flash cards, and then invite students to read them aloud with you. Challenge volunteers to write the words on the board. If they get stuck, encourage them to sound out the word, and then show them the flash card, or invite classmates to help them if they continue to have difficulty.

2 Ask volunteers to use each sports word in a sentence. Encourage students to add interesting details, including whether or not they like to play or watch this sport, where they play (or watch) it, or someone they know who enjoys the sport. For example, a student might say *I like to watch the Red Sox play baseball at Fenway Park* or *My Aunt Barbara likes to play tennis.*

3 Invite students to name sports they enjoy playing at school, and record their responses on the board. Have the class vote on their two favorite sports. Display the All-Star Sports overhead transparency. Record facts about those two sports.

4 Display the My Favorite Sports overhead transparency. Invite the class to help you complete the sentences. On a blank transparency, draw two circles the same size as the ones on the reproducible to make the second page for each sport. Write information about each sport and its equipment on the second circle. Draw another circle on a blank transparency to make the book's cover. Write *Room ___'s Favorite Sports*, and decorate it to look like one of the balls from the favorite sports or draw a scene of one of those sports being played.

Independent Practice

1 Give each student an All-Star Sports reproducible. Ask students to choose their two favorite sports. Encourage them to look at the lists you recorded in Setting the Stage and Instructional Input. Have them fill in as many details as they can about the two sports.

2 Write the sentence frames from the My Favorite Sports reproducible on the board or sentence strips, or display the transparency. Have students complete the sentence frames based on their two favorite sports. Remind them to write information about each sport and its equipment after they complete each sentence frame.

3 Have students revise and edit their rough draft and then use the rubric to evaluate their writing.

Presentation

- Have students **publish** their final drafts on the My Favorite Sports reproducibles. Have them draw second circles for each sport and write about the sport and its equipment inside the circles.
- Invite students to **create** front covers by drawing a circle, writing ___*'s Favorite Sports* as the title, and decorating it as a sports ball or with a scene of one of the sports being played. Tell students to cut out all of their circles, and bind their book with a metal ring or yarn through a hole in the top of the book.
- Encourage students to **share** their books with classmates.

TEACHING HINTS/EXTENSIONS

- Take a class vote to determine the top two favorite sports played by professional athletes. Create a bar graph to illustrate the results.
- Create a sports learning center that includes books about sports, sports equipment, sports cards, and student trophies and ribbons. Encourage students to cut out sports articles and pictures from the newspaper or magazines to add to the center.

- Divide the class into two teams. Invite students to name their teams. Designate four spots in the room to represent the bases on a baseball field. Have the first "batter" stand at home plate. Ask him or her to answer a simple math word problem related to sports or to spell a sports-related word. If the student answers correctly, have him or her advance to first base. If the student is incorrect, he or she is out. After three outs, the other team gets to bat. Because of time constraints, you may want to limit this game to three or four innings.
- Have students complete one or more of these writing prompts in a journal:
  - ✔ Tell about the best sports game you ever watched.
  - ✔ Tell about the best sports game you ever played in.
  - ✔ Write about a sport you don't like and explain why you don't like it.

Name ______________________ Date ______________________

Sports Word Recognition

Directions: Fill in the bubble next to the name of the correct sport.

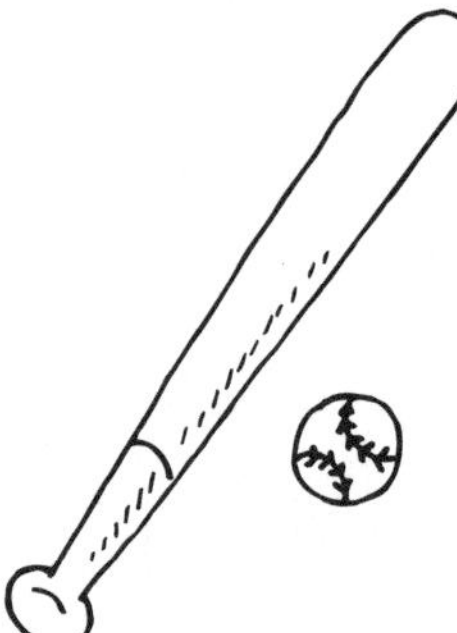	○ volleyball ○ baseball ○ basketball		○ baseball ○ tennis ○ football
	○ basketball ○ swimming ○ soccer	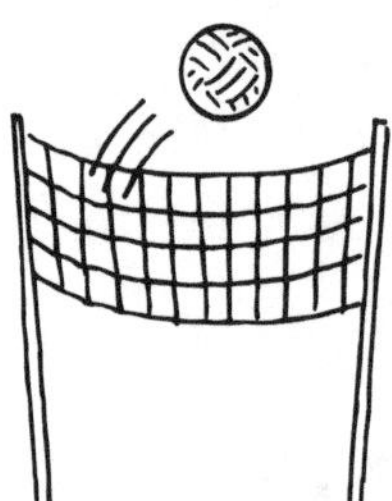	○ volleyball ○ basketball ○ soccer
	○ skiing ○ volleyball ○ tennis	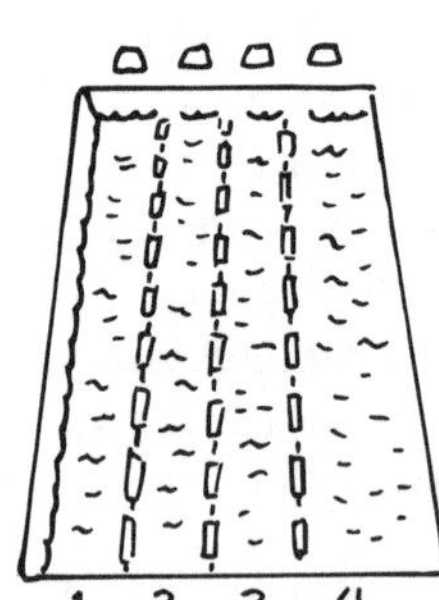	○ basketball ○ swimming ○ baseball
	○ swimming ○ soccer ○ football	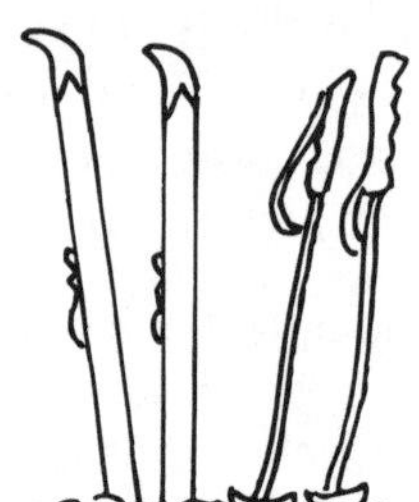	○ skiing ○ swimming ○ football

Name ______________________ Date ______________________

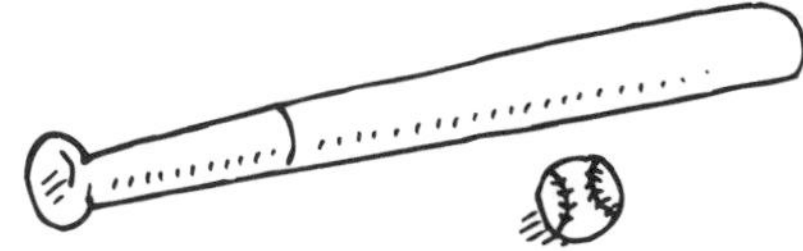

All-Star Sports

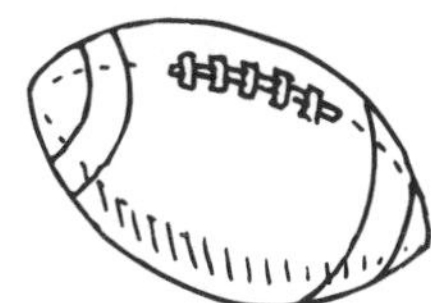

Sport 1	Sport 2
What equipment is needed?	
1. ________	1. ________
2. ________	2. ________
3. ________	3. ________
4. ________	4. ________
5. ________	5. ________
How do you play?	
1. ________	1. ________
2. ________	2. ________
3. ________	3. ________
4. ________	4. ________
5. ________	5. ________
Why do you like it?	
1. ________	1. ________
2. ________	2. ________
3. ________	3. ________
4. ________	4. ________
5. ________	5. ________

My Favorite Sports

My favorite sport is

____

because when I ____________________________
(play, watch)

I ____________________________,

____________________________, and

____________________________.

My next favorite sport is

____

because when I ____________________________
(play, watch)

I ____________________________,

____________________________, and

____________________________.

Let's Celebrate

Preparation

Read aloud books about celebrations.

- *The Flying Latke* by Arthur Yorinks (Simon & Schuster)
- *I'm in Charge of Celebrations* by Byrd Baylor (Aladdin)
- *Lion Dancer: Ernie Wan's Chinese New Year* by Kate Waters and Madeline Slovenz-low (Scholastic)

Gather several pieces of chart paper and a 12-month calendar.

Make copies of these reproducibles.

- Celebration Word Recognition (page 148) transparency, class set of photocopies
- Favorite Celebration (page 149) transparency, class set of photocopies
- Let's Celebrate (page 150) transparency, class set of photocopies
- rubric (page 9) class set of photocopies

Setting the Stage

Divide a piece of chart paper into eight sections. Draw simple symbols in each section to represent the following celebrations: Chanukah, birthday, Christmas, Halloween, Thanksgiving, Valentine's Day, Cinco de Mayo, and Fourth of July. Invite students to identify what holiday or celebration each set of symbols represents. Write the names of the holidays and celebrations under the symbols. Encourage students to use this chart as a word bank as they write throughout the lesson.

OBJECTIVE

The student will write several sentences about his or her favorite celebration.

CRITICAL COMPONENTS

- Sentences identify the student's favorite celebration.
- Sentences include details about why this celebration is the student's favorite.
- Each sentence and each proper noun begin with a capital letter.
- Each sentence ends with the correct punctuation.

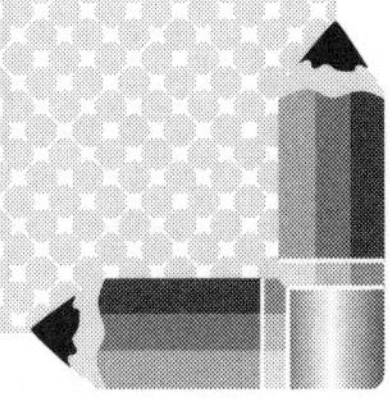

Instructional Input

1 Briefly discuss each holiday and celebration on the chart from Setting the Stage. Discuss the significance of each symbol. Label the symbols as they are discussed. Add additional pictures and phrases as students share information. Ask students when each is celebrated, and record this information on a calendar.

2 Tell students your favorite celebration. Give several reasons why it is your favorite. For example, you might say *My favorite celebration is Thanksgiving. I like saying thank you to my family and my friends for everything I have. I also like it because I eat a big feast of turkey, stuffing, potatoes, vegetables, and pumpkin pie. My favorite part is being with my family and telling them I love them.* Invite students to share their favorite holiday and one reason why they like it.

3 Give each student a Celebration Word Recognition reproducible. Invite volunteers to identify what holiday is celebrated with the items in each box. Say several sentences about each holiday. For example, say *Chanukah is celebrated in December. Chanukah is a holiday that lasts for eight days. Jewish people celebrate Chanukah.* Tell students to fill in the bubble next to the name of the holiday.

4 Display the Celebration Word Recognition overhead transparency. Review the correct answers, and have students circle them.

Guided Practice

1 Invite students to brainstorm a list of celebrations and details about them such as when, why, and how they are celebrated. Record their responses on separate pieces of chart paper.

2 Display the Favorite Celebration overhead transparency. Complete the sentence with the name of the celebration you said was your favorite during the Instructional Input activity. Invite students to help you list information about it.

Valentine's Day

- February 14
- to say I love you
- give cards
- buy flowers
- celebrates a saint
- get heart candy
- eat chocolate

3 Display the Let's Celebrate overhead transparency. Have students help you write several sentences about your favorite celebration. Encourage them to use the information you recorded on the Favorite Celebration transparency as well as the word bank from Setting the Stage and the lists of celebrations.

4 Give each student a Favorite Celebration reproducible. Encourage students to complete the reproducible based on their favorite celebration.

Independent Practice

1 Have students write several sentences about their favorite celebration. Remind them to use the information they recorded on the Favorite Celebration reproducible as well as the word bank and lists you recorded during the lesson.

2 Have students revise and edit their rough draft and then use the rubric to evaluate their writing.

Presentation

- Have students **publish** their final drafts on the Let's Celebrate reproducibles.
- Invite students to **draw** illustrations of the celebrations, and mount them on construction paper.
- **Display** student work on a bulletin board in the order the celebrations occur throughout the year (e.g., New Year's Day is followed by Valentine's Day).
- **Create** a class book titled *We Celebrate!* by attaching students' writing to the back of their mounted illustrations. Bind the pages with fancy ribbon.

TEACHING HINTS/EXTENSIONS

- Bring in items or display pictures that represent holiday celebrations. Discuss the use of each item and its significance. Encourage students to add to the display.
- Many celebrations originated in other places (e.g., Kwanzaa: Africa; Chanukah: Israel; Cinco de Mayo: Mexico; Christmas: Europe). Locate and label these countries on a world map.
- Extend students' vocabulary by having them create acrostic poems for different holidays. Write the holiday vertically on the board or a large piece of paper. Then, have students brainstorm an appropriate word or phrase for each letter.

- Have students complete one or more of these writing prompts in a journal:
  - ✔ Pretend you are throwing a party and your grandparents aren't able to come. Write them a letter convincing them to attend.
  - ✔ It is your favorite holiday today. What day is it? What traditions will you follow?
  - ✔ Nominate a day for a holiday. What is the name of the holiday and why do you want to celebrate it?

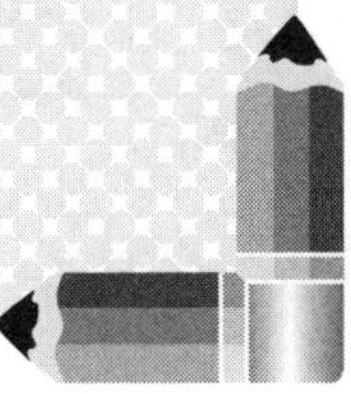

Name ______________________________ Date ______________________

Celebration Word Recognition

Directions: Fill in the bubble next to the name of the holiday.

○ Valentine's Day
○ birthday
○ Fourth of July

○ birthday
○ Cinco de Mayo
○ Thanksgiving

○ Halloween
○ Cinco de Mayo
○ Christmas

○ Valentine's Day
○ birthday
○ Christmas

○ Halloween
○ Fourth of July
○ Chanukah

○ Thanksgiving
○ Cinco de Mayo
○ Halloween

○ Christmas
○ Halloween
○ Chanukah

○ Fourth of July
○ Christmas
○ Thanksgiving

Name ______________________ Date ______________________

Favorite Celebration

My favorite celebration is ______________________.

I celebrate with	I like to eat
I like to	It's my favorite celebration because

Name ______________________________ Date ______________________

Let's Celebrate

Rainbow Writing

Preparation

Read aloud books about colors.

- *Color* by Ruth Heller (Puffin)
- *The Color Box* by Dayle Ann Dodds (Little, Brown and Company)
- *The Mixed-up Chameleon* by Eric Carle (Ty Crowell)

Gather three to five pieces of chart paper and a timer.

Collect one piece of blue, red, pink, green, orange, white, and purple construction paper and a class set of construction paper (any color).

Make copies of these reproducibles.
- Color Word Recognition (page 154) transparency, class set of photocopies
- Favorite Colors Booklet (page 155) transparency, class set of photocopies
- A Colorful World (page 156) transparency, class set of photocopies
- rubric (page 9) class set of photocopies

Setting the Stage

Choose a color (a different color than the construction paper you will hand out), and write it on a piece of chart paper. Set a timer for 2 minutes, and ask students to brainstorm objects that are that color. Record their responses on the chart paper. Repeat this process for one or two more colors (different colors than the construction paper colors you will hand out) to create color word banks. Then, divide the class into seven groups, give each group a piece of colored construction paper, and have each group generate a list of objects the same color as their paper. Invite each group to share their list with the class, and post all the color word banks on the wall. Encourage students to add words to the lists.

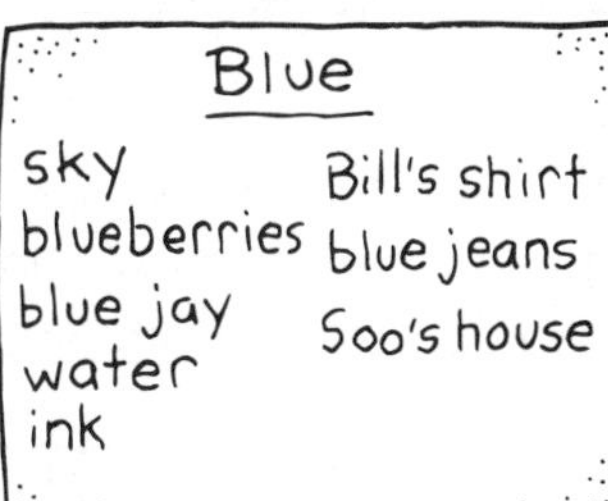

OBJECTIVE

The student will write several sentences about his or her favorite colors.

CRITICAL COMPONENTS

- Sentences identify favorite colors.
- Sentences include details about why these are the student's favorite colors.
- Each sentence and each proper noun begin with a capital letter.
- Each sentence ends with the correct punctuation.

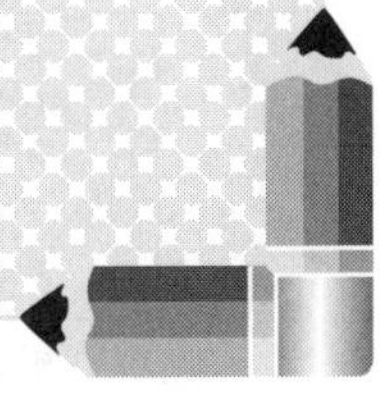

Instructional Input

1 Tell students why you like your favorite color. For example, you might say *My favorite color is yellow because it is bright and cheerful. I always feel happy when I wear yellow or am in a yellow room. Yellow also reminds me of daffodils and sunflowers, which are my two favorite flowers.* Write the reasons on a piece of chart paper.

2 Ask each student to share his or her favorite color and one reason why. Record all the colors and reasons on a piece of chart paper. Have students brainstorm additional colors and reasons they like them.

3 Give each student a Color Word Recognition reproducible. Invite volunteers to identify the object in each box. Discuss what color the object in the picture is. Compare it to other objects that are the same color. For example, say *Red is the color of apples. Red is also the color of fire trucks and stop signs. My favorite flowers are red roses.* Tell students to fill in the bubble next to the color of the object in the picture.

4 Display the Color Word Recognition overhead transparency. Review the correct answers, and have students circle them.

Guided Practice

1 Display the Favorite Colors Booklet overhead transparency. Ask students to help you complete the sentence frames. For example, you might write *My favorite color is <u>blue</u> because it is the color of <u>the ocean</u> and <u>Cookie Monster</u>.* If students need help with ideas or vocabulary, encourage them to refer to the lists and word banks you recorded in Setting the Stage and Instructional Input.

2 Display the A Colorful World overhead transparency. Have students help you write about at least two favorite colors. Include information about why the colors are your favorite, what objects the colors remind you of, and how the colors make you feel.

3 Give each student a Favorite Colors Booklet reproducible. Have students complete the sentence frames based on their two favorite colors. Photocopy additional reproducibles for students who want to write about more than two colors.

4 Invite students to make front and back covers by cutting out the crayon shapes, tracing them on construction paper, and cutting out their tracings. Then, have them staple all their pages together to make individual books.

Independent Practice

1 Have students write about at least two colors that are their favorites. Tell them to name the colors, tell why the colors are their favorites, what objects the colors remind them of, and how the colors make them feel. Encourage students to refer to their completed Favorite Colors Booklet and the lists and word banks you recorded. Invite students who have a difficult time writing independently to begin by copying the sentences they completed on their Favorite Colors Booklet.

2 Have students revise and edit their rough draft and then use the rubric to evaluate their writing.

Presentation

- Have students **publish** their final drafts on the A Colorful World reproducibles.
- **Host** a "Favorite Color Day" in your classroom. Invite students to wear their favorite color and bring a snack that is their favorite color to share with the class.
- Encourage students to **share** their final drafts on Favorite Color Day.

TEACHING HINTS/EXTENSIONS

- Explain to students that when sunlight shines through drops of water, the light is bent and splits into seven colors. Tell them that each color has its own wavelength, which explains why the colors in a rainbow are always in the same order. Explain that red has the longest wavelength so it is always on the outside edge and violet has the shortest wavelength so it is always on the inside edge. Encourage students to keep their eyes open for rainbows. Hang a prism in a sunny window, bring in abalone shells, turn on a sprinkler on a sunny day, or give students bubble mixture to observe rainbows.

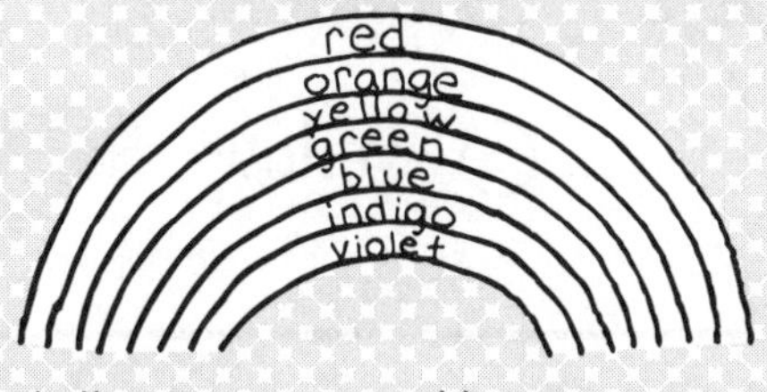

- Help students remember that the colors of a rainbow are always in the same order by introducing them to *Roy G. Biv* (**r**ed, **o**range, **y**ellow, **g**reen, **b**lue, **i**ndigo, **v**iolet). The letters in his name represent the correct order of the colors of a rainbow. Pin yarn to a bulletin board to represent the arcs of a rainbow. Label each arc with the appropriate color. Give students magazines, old wallpaper books, catalogs, and fabric swatches. Invite students to look for items in each color category and pin them to the bulletin board.
- Invite students to vote on their favorite color. Choose the top two responses, and take the class on a scavenger hunt around the school and surrounding neighborhood to locate and record items that are the chosen colors.
- Have students complete one or more of these writing prompts in a journal:
  - ✔ If you could design your own bedroom, what would it look like? What colors would you use?
  - ✔ Design your own bicycle. What would it look like? What colors would you use?
  - ✔ Design your own lunch box or backpack. What would it look like? What colors would be on it?

Name ______________________________ Date ______________________________

Color Word Recognition

Directions: Fill in the bubble next to the color of the object in the picture.

- ○ orange
- ○ red
- ○ purple

- ○ purple
- ○ white
- ○ red

- ○ red
- ○ blue
- ○ yellow

- ○ green
- ○ brown
- ○ purple

- ○ black
- ○ yellow
- ○ white

- ○ white
- ○ green
- ○ orange

- ○ white
- ○ green
- ○ orange

- ○ yellow
- ○ brown
- ○ purple

Favorite Colors Booklet

My favorite color is ______________

because it is the color of ______________

____

and ______________.

My next favorite color is ______________

because it is the color of ______________

____

and ______________.

Name ______________________________ Date ______________________________

A Colorful World

White
cloud
bunny
snow
cotton
marshmallow

Red
tulip
watermelon
fire engine
stop sign
apple
fire

Blue
pond
sky
blueberry
lake
bluebird

Green
grass
tree
grape

On the Move

Preparation

Read aloud books about different modes of transportation.

- *I Fly* by Anne Rockwell (Crown Books)
- *The Little Auto* by Lois Lenski (Random House Books)
- *Minton Goes Sailing* by Anna Fienberg (Allen & Unwin)

Gather a piece of construction paper for each student and three to five pieces of chart paper.

Make copies of these reproducibles.
- Transportation Word Recognition (page 160) transparency, class set of photocopies
- Car Travel Book (page 161) transparency, class set of photocopies
- Travel Time (page 162) transparency, class set of photocopies
- rubric (page 9) class set of photocopies

Setting the Stage

Divide a piece of chart paper into eight sections. Write several clue words in each section for the following modes of transportation: car, boat, bus, truck, airplane, motorcycle, train, and hot air balloon. Say each word as you write it. For example, for train write and say *tracks, conductor,* and *whistle* or for boat write and say *water, sail,* and *anchor.* Invite students to identify what mode of transportation each set of clues describes. Write the name of the mode of transportation under the clue words. Ask students to brainstorm other modes of transportation. Remind them to include methods that can be used by students such as walking and bicycles. Record their responses on a separate piece of chart paper or on index cards or sentence strips to create a word bank.

OBJECTIVE

The student will write several sentences about his or her favorite mode of transportation.

CRITICAL COMPONENTS

- Sentences identify a favorite mode of transportation.
- Sentences include details about why the student likes this mode of transportation.
- Each sentence and each proper noun begin with a capital letter.
- Each sentence ends with the correct punctuation.

Instructional Input

1 Share several of the ways you have traveled and some interesting experiences you have had. Tell students what your favorite way to travel is and why it is your favorite. For example, you might say *My favorite way to travel is by boat. A boat can take me to new, interesting places. I love to be on the ocean and feel the ocean breeze.* Write your mode of transportation on a piece of chart paper, and list the information below it.

Airplane	Train
I'm up high.	I see many new things.
I go fast.	I hear the whistle blow.
I can see movies.	I like to eat in the dining car.
Cars and people look small.	It goes fast.

2 Ask each student to share his or her favorite way to travel and two reasons why. Encourage students to choose a way they would like to travel even if they haven't experienced it yet. Record each mode of transportation and the reasons students like it on several pieces of chart paper.

3 Give each student a Transportation Word Recognition reproducible. Invite volunteers to identify the mode of transportation in each box. Say several sentences about each mode of transportation. For example, say *A motorcycle has two wheels. My whole family can not fit on a motorcycle. Sometimes, a motorcycle is black.* Tell students to fill in the bubble next to the word that identifies the mode of transportation.

4 Display the Transportation Word Recognition overhead transparency. Review the correct answers, and have students circle them.

Guided Practice

1 Invite students to explain why they like to ride in cars. Encourage them to think of things they do in the car, things they see while they are in the car, and ways they feel when they are in the car traveling somewhere.

2 Display the Car Travel Book overhead transparency. Read aloud the sentence frame. Invite students to help you complete the sentence (e.g., *I like to travel by car because in a car I play games, sing songs, and see buildings*). If students need help with ideas or vocabulary, encourage them to refer to the lists and word banks you recorded in Setting the Stage and Instructional Input. On the second car shape, write additional information about why students like to ride in cars.

3 Display the Travel Time overhead transparency. Invite students to help you write about your favorite mode of transportation. Include information about why you like it, what you do while you are in it, what you see while you ride in it, where you go in it, and how you feel when you are in it.

4 Give each student a Car Travel Book reproducible. Have students complete the sentence frame and write additional information about why they like to ride in cars. Have students make front and back covers by cutting out the car shapes, tracing them on construction paper, and cutting out their tracings. Then, have them staple all their pages together to make individual books.

Independent Practice

1 Have students write several sentences about their favorite mode of transportation. Have them include information about why they like it, where they go and what they see while they are in it, what they do while they travel in it, and how it makes them feel. Encourage them to refer to the lists and word banks you recorded.

2 Have students revise and edit their rough draft and then use the rubric to evaluate their writing.

Presentation

- Have students **publish** their final drafts on the Travel Time reproducibles.
- Encourage students to **share** their final drafts with the whole class or in small groups.
- **Display** student work on a bulletin board decorated with maps and travel brochures.
- **Create** a class book of students' writing.

TEACHING HINTS/EXTENSIONS

- Make a transportation graph with symbols that represent the modes of transportation the class discussed in the lesson. Survey students to see the various ways they have traveled. Record the results on the graph. Ask questions about the graph, and encourage students to generate additional questions. For example, ask *How many more students have traveled by bus than by airplane? What is the total number of students who have traveled by truck and train?*

How Have You Traveled?

How Many?

20
15
10
5

car | boat | train | plane | balloon

Mode of Transportation

- Ask students to brainstorm songs they know or have heard that are related to transportation. Invite the music teacher or a parent volunteer to lead the class in a "Travel Sing-Along." Possible songs include "The Wheels on the Bus," "I've Been Working on the Railroad," "Down by the Station," and "Row, Row, Row Your Boat."
- Provide additional writing experiences by inviting students to write a story with a title such as *The Best Trip I Ever Took, The Runaway Train,* or *If I Could Fly Anywhere I Would Go . . . .*
- Have students complete one or more of these writing prompts in a journal:
  - ✔ Convince someone who doesn't like to fly to take an airplane trip.
  - ✔ Convince someone who is afraid of water to take a cruise on a boat.
  - ✔ Convince someone who has never been on a bus to ride a bus across town.

Name ______________________ Date ______________________

Transportation Word Recognition

Directions: Fill in the bubble next to the word that identifies the mode of transportation.

○ can
○ car
○ carnival

○ bone
○ bat
○ boat

○ bus
○ bump
○ bass

○ trick
○ try
○ truck

○ ape
○ airport
○ airplane

○ mouse
○ motorcycle
○ morning

○ truck
○ train
○ tray

○ hot air balloon
○ hotel
○ helmet

Car Travel Book

I like to travel by car because in a car I ______________________,
______________________ ______________________
______________________, and ______________________.

Name ______________________ Date ______________________

Travel Time

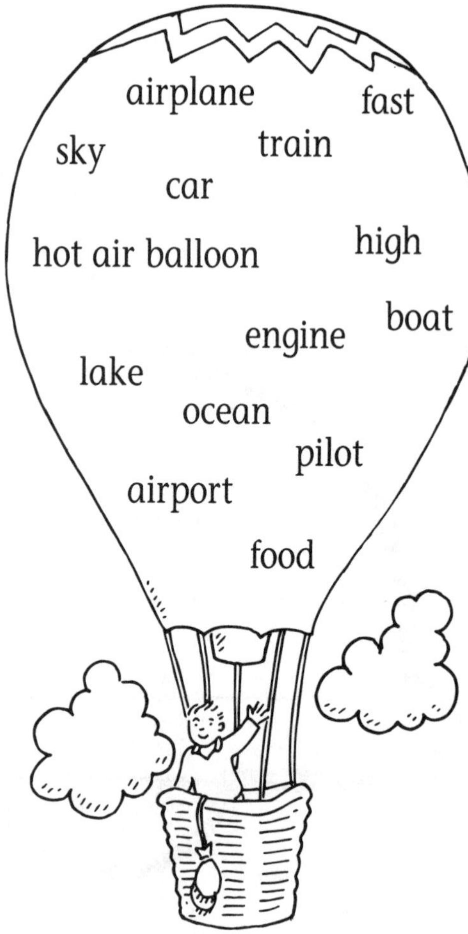

airplane
fast
sky
train
car
hot air balloon
high
boat
engine
lake
ocean
pilot
airport
food

Helping Hands

Preparation

Read aloud books about community helpers.

- *Career Day* by Anne Rockwell (HarperCollins)
- *Community Helpers from A–Z* by Bobbie Kalman (Crabtree)
- *I Want to Be a Firefighter* (The "I Want to Be" Series) (Firefly Books)

Invite one or more community helpers to visit your classroom and bring tools they use in their job.

Gather two or three pieces of chart paper.

Make copies of these reproducibles.
- Career Word Recognition (page 166) transparency, class set of photocopies
- career book template (page 167) transparency, class set of photocopies
- rubric (page 9) class set of photocopies

Setting the Stage

Have one or more community helpers speak to your class and discuss their careers. Ask them to stress the aspects of their careers that are of service to the public and show tools they use in their job. Invite students to ask questions. After the community helpers have left, have students draw pictures of each of them at work. Compile each set of pictures and a thank-you letter into a book, and send each book to the appropriate person.

OBJECTIVE

The student will write several sentences about a community helper.

CRITICAL COMPONENTS

- Sentences identify a community helper career choice.
- Sentences include details about why the student would like this career.
- Each sentence and each proper noun begin with a capital letter.
- Each sentence ends with the correct punctuation.

Instructional Input

1 List the jobs of the guest speakers on a piece of chart paper. Ask students to recall some of the duties each guest performed, and record their responses below each job title.

2 Ask students to brainstorm additional jobs that serve people. Tell students that workers with these jobs are often called community helpers because they help the people in the community in a special way. Record each job on the chart paper along with additional information students know about it. (List a teacher, but do not record information about a teacher until you get to Guided Practice.)

Firefighter	Letter Carrier
puts out fires	sorts letters
cleans the firehouse	delivers letters
rescues trapped people	drives a truck

3 Give each student a Career Word Recognition reproducible. Invite volunteers to identify which community helper would use the items in each box. Say several sentences about each community helper. For example, say *A bus driver helps people get to different places. I see the bus driver every morning when I go to school. My bus driver is named Ralph.* Tell students to fill in the bubble next to the name of the community helper who would use the items in the picture.

4 Display the Career Word Recognition overhead transparency. Review the correct answers, and have students circle them.

Guided Practice

1 Draw a web on a piece of chart paper. Write *teacher* in the central circle. Ask students to help you brainstorm ideas about what a teacher does and how a teacher helps other people.

2 Display the career book template overhead transparency. Read aloud the sentence frames. Invite students to help you complete these sentences to describe your job as a teacher. Encourage them to refer to the web, word banks, and lists you recorded in Instructional Input. Invite students to read aloud the completed sentences with you.

3 Have students tell what community helper career they would like to have when they grow up. Encourage them to tell one or two reasons why they would like to have this job.

Independent Practice

1 Write the sentence frames from the career book reproducible on the board or on sentence strips, or display the transparency. Have students copy them and complete the sentences. Invite students to write additional sentences about why they want that career and how they will help people.

2 Have students revise and edit their rough draft and then use the rubric to evaluate their writing.

Presentation

- Have students **publish** their final drafts on the career book template reproducibles. Tell them to fold their paper (inwards) on the dotted line to form individual books and write a title and their name on the front cover.
- Invite students to **draw** illustrations in the boxes on the template and decorate the book cover.
- Encourage students to **share** their books with the class and dress up as community helpers.

TEACHING HINTS/EXTENSIONS

- Bring in various tools, hats, and pieces of clothing that could be worn by a community helper (e.g., stethoscope, letters, chalk, books, bandages, flashlight). Place the items in a box. Invite students to take out one tool or article of clothing and tell about the job it represents.
- Create a class mural titled *Our Hardworking Parents*. Invite each student to draw and color a parent at work, cut it out, and place it on the mural. Label each picture with the parent's name and job. Invite parents to share their job and specific job skills with the class.

- Invite students to make thank-you cards to distribute to various community helpers in the neighborhood. Have students use the following sentence frame: *Thank you ____________ for ____________. I appreciate you!*
- Have students complete one or more of these writing prompts in a journal:
  - ✔ Pretend you are firefighter. Write about your day.
  - ✔ Pretend you are a police officer. Write about your day.
  - ✔ Pretend you are a doctor. Write about your day.

Name ______________________ Date ______________________

Career Word Recognition

Directions: Fill in the bubble next to the name of the community helper who would use the items in the picture.

- ○ letter carrier
- ○ teacher
- ○ forest ranger

- ○ nurse
- ○ firefighter
- ○ police officer

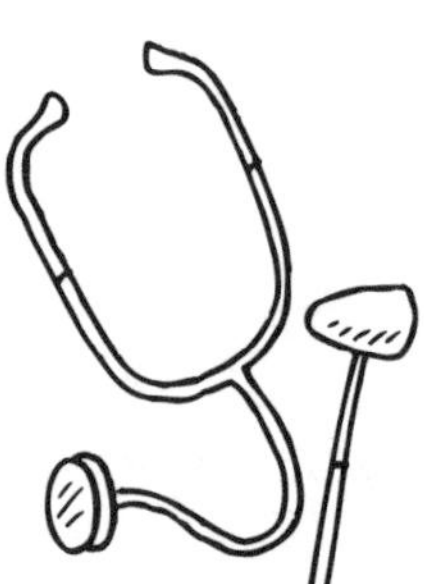

- ○ police officer
- ○ bus driver
- ○ doctor

- ○ forest ranger
- ○ letter carrier
- ○ doctor

- ○ police officer
- ○ letter carrier
- ○ nurse

- ○ nurse
- ○ teacher
- ○ letter carrier

- ○ forest ranger
- ○ firefighter
- ○ teacher

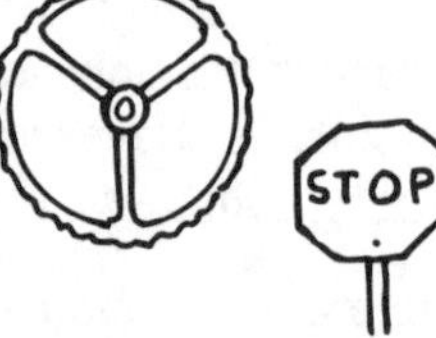

- ○ bus driver
- ○ teacher
- ○ forest ranger

The best career is ______________________

because if you are a ______________________

you can ______________________.

You can also ______________________,

______________________,

and ______________________.

Yummy

Preparation

Read aloud books about food.

- *Growing Vegetable Soup* by Lois Ehlert (Harcourt)
- *Never Take a Pig to Lunch: And Other Poems About the Fun of Eating* by Nadine Bernard Wescott (Orchard Books)
- *Yummy! Eating Through a Day* by Lee Bennett Hopkins (Simon & Schuster)

Gather a file folder, a brass fastener, and felt or yarn for the teacher and each student; chart paper; five magazines; and five pieces of construction paper.

Make copies of these reproducibles.
- Food Word Recognition (page 171) transparency, class set of photocopies
- I Like to Eat! (page 172) transparency, two class sets of photocopies
- Head with Movable Mouth (page 173) teacher photocopy and class set of photocopies on card stock
- rubric (page 9) class set of photocopies

Prepare a sample My Favorite Foods file folder book. (See Guided Practice.)

Setting the Stage

Write *Fruit, Vegetable, Bread, Meat,* and *Dessert* on a piece of chart paper. Share with the class your favorite food from each category, and write each food under the appropriate heading. Talk about why these foods are your favorites. For example, you might say *Baby carrots are my favorite vegetable because they are crunchy and sweet.* Have each student name his or her favorite food, identify which heading it belongs under, and tell why it is his or her favorite. As students name various foods, add them to the word bank on the chart paper.

OBJECTIVE

The student will write several sentences about his or her favorite foods.

CRITICAL COMPONENTS

- Sentences identify the student's favorite foods .
- Sentences include details about why these foods are the student's favorites.
- Each sentence and each proper noun begin with a capital letter.
- Each sentence ends with the correct punctuation.

Instructional Input

1 Divide the class into five groups. Give each group a magazine and a sheet of construction paper. Assign each group a different category of food: fruit, vegetable, bread, meat, or dessert. Have students find pictures of food in their category, cut them out, glue them onto the construction paper, and label them.

2 Invite each group to share their collage with the class. Ask them to name their food category and the foods on their collage. Post the collages on the wall for students to use as word banks as they write throughout the lesson.

3 Give each student a Food Word Recognition reproducible. Invite volunteers to identify the food in each box. Say several sentences about each food item. For example, say *I like to eat ice cream when it is hot outside. My favorite flavor of ice cream is chocolate. I like to eat ice cream in a cone.* Tell students to fill in the bubble next to the name of the food.

4 Display the Food Word Recognition overhead transparency. Review the correct answers, and have students circle them.

Guided Practice

1 Show students the sample My Favorite Foods file folder book you prepared. Give each student a Head with Movable Mouth reproducible, a file folder, a brass fastener, felt or yarn, and art supplies.

2 Use your sample to demonstrate how students will make their book. Tell students to write *My Favorite Foods* and their name along the front of the folder.

3 Tell students to cut out the head and mouth piece. Have them place the brass fastener through the circle on the mouth piece and through the circle on the head. (The mouth should be able to move up and down to eat.) Show them how to glue or staple the head (not the mouth) to one side of the inside of the folder. Invite them to add "hair" with felt or yarn.

4 Display the I Like to Eat! overhead transparency. Read aloud the sentence frames. Ask students to help you complete the sentences for two different food categories. For example, you might write *I like to eat many different foods. My favorite* <u>*fruit*</u> *is* <u>*a banana*</u>*. This food is my favorite because* <u>*it is fun to take the peel off and eat the inside*</u>. If students need help with ideas or vocabulary, encourage them to refer to the word banks you recorded in Setting the Stage and the collages they created in Instructional Input. Read aloud the completed sentences. (These pages will go in the My Favorite Foods file folder book.)

Independent Practice

1 Give each student an I Like to Eat! reproducible for their rough draft. Have students write about two favorite foods from different food categories. Photocopy additional reproducibles for students who want to write about more than two favorite foods.

2 Have students revise and edit their rough draft and then use the rubric to evaluate their writing.

Presentation

- Have students **publish** their final drafts on the I Like to Eat! reproducibles. Staple them to the inside flap opposite their head in their My Favorite Foods file folder books.
- Encourage students to **share** their file folder books with classmates, parents, and other classes.
- **Display** the folders in the classroom library.

TEACHING HINTS/EXTENSIONS

- Invite students to bring their favorite fruit to class. Have them tell why the fruit is their favorite. Make a chart on the board to record the names of the fruits and how many people brought each fruit. Teach students to make a tally mark for each fruit in groups of five. Invite students to count by fives. Make a graph to illustrate the results.
- Bring several ripe avocados, dip mix, and tortilla chips to class. Make guacamole dip for the class to try. Talk about the large seed inside this fruit, and let the seed sprout by placing the bottom of it in a cup of water. Encourage students to keep track of the plant growth by drawing pictures, labeling parts, and writing sentences about it.
- Take the class on a tour of a local farmer's market or nearby grocery store. Ask an employee to tell the class about his or her favorite foods. Purchase a small bag of popcorn kernels, and make popcorn when you return to the classroom. Encourage students to talk about what favorite foods they saw on the tour. Invite them to write a thank-you note to the employee you spoke with, the manager, or the owner.

- Have students complete one or more of these writing prompts in a journal:
  - ✔ Describe your favorite dinner.
  - ✔ Describe the most delicious lunch you have ever had.
  - ✔ Describe the best breakfast in the world.

Name ______________________________ Date ____________________

Food Word Recognition

Directions: Fill in the bubble next to the name of the food.

○ apple
○ ape
○ animal

○ munch
○ muffin
○ mitten

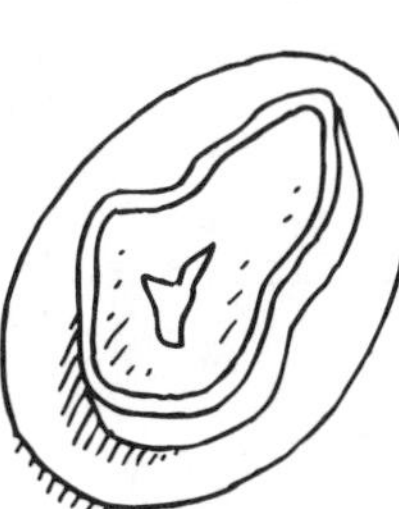

○ stop
○ steak
○ sack

○ car
○ carrots
○ cats

○ cone
○ carrots
○ cookies

○ icicle
○ ice cube
○ ice cream

○ bread
○ break
○ bride

○ garage
○ grapes
○ great

Name ______________________________ Date ______________________

I Like to Eat!

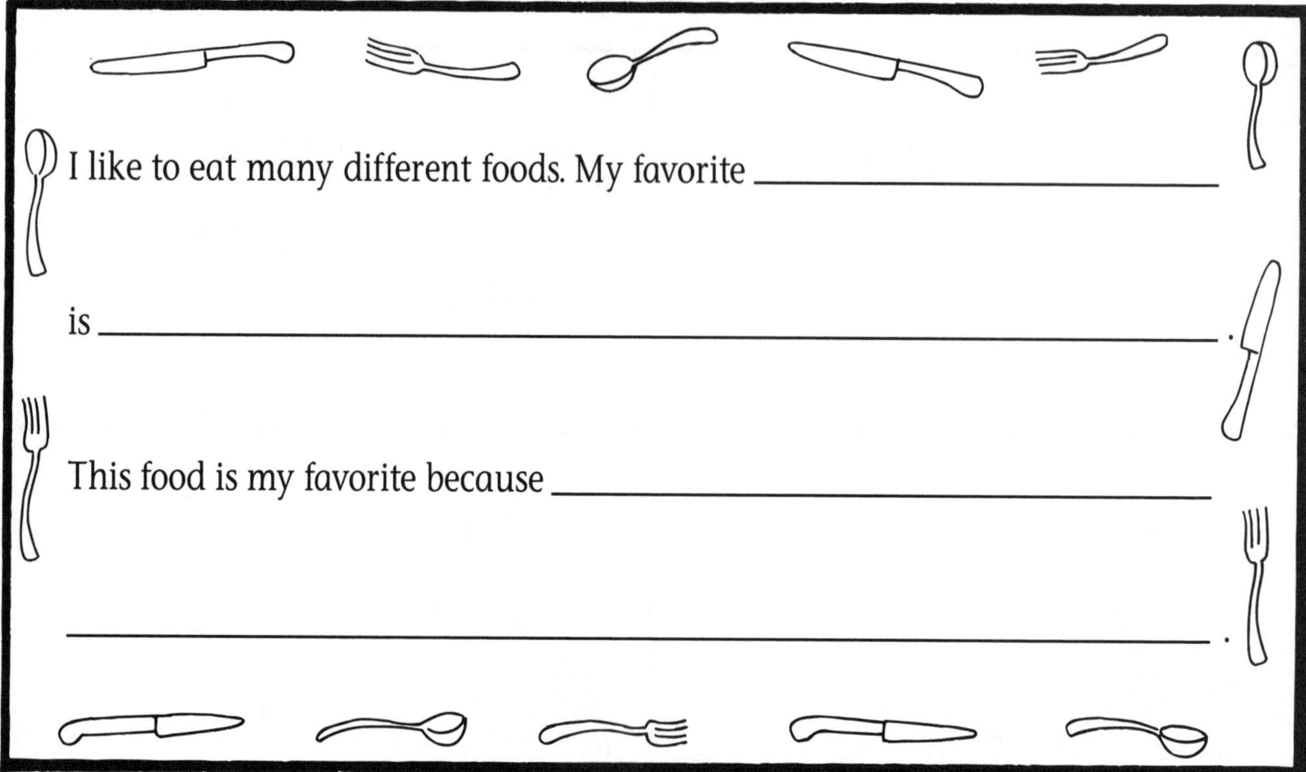

I like to eat many different foods. My favorite ____________________

is ____.

This food is my favorite because ______________________________

____.

I like to eat many different foods. My favorite ____________________

is ____.

This food is my favorite because ______________________________

____.

Name ______________________________ Date ______________________________

Head with Movable Mouth

Directions: Cut out the head and the mouth piece. Insert a brass fastener through the circle on the mouth piece and through the circle on the head to make the mouth move. Glue or staple the head (not the mouth) to one side of the inside of your folder. Add hair with felt or yarn.

Playtime

Preparation

Read aloud books about toys.

- *My Friend Harry* by Kim Lewis (Candlewick Press)
- *The Velveteen Rabbit* by Margery Williams (Doubleday Books)
- *Where Are You, Blue Kangaroo?* by Emma Chichester Clark (Doubleday Books)

Gather a piece of string 10 inches (25.5 cm) long for the teacher and each student and chart paper.

Bring a ball in a paper bag to class on the first day of the lesson.

Make copies of these reproducibles.

- Favorite Toys (page 177) transparency, class set of photocopies
- Toy Word Recognition (page 178) transparency, class set of photocopies
- Toy Suitcase Pattern (page 179) two teacher photocopies and two class sets of photocopies on card stock
- Pack Your Toy Suitcase (page 180) transparency, class set of photocopies
- rubric (page 9) class set of photocopies

Prepare a sample toy suitcase. (See Guided Practice.)

Setting the Stage

Hold up the paper bag with the ball hidden inside. Tell the class that you have brought a favorite toy to show. Pantomime playing with a ball, and invite students to guess what is in the bag. Invite the class to brainstorm a word bank of toys. Record their responses on a piece of chart paper. Have several volunteers pantomime playing with toys from the word bank.

OBJECTIVE

The student will write several sentences about his or her favorite toys.

CRITICAL COMPONENTS

- Sentences identify the student's favorite toys.
- Sentences include details about why these toys are the student's favorites.
- Each sentence and each proper noun begin with a capital letter.
- Each sentence ends with the correct punctuation.

Instructional Input

1 Give each student a Favorite Toys reproducible, and display the overhead transparency. Read aloud the story, and then invite the class to read it aloud with you.

2 Tell students to fill in the bubbles next to the toys that Mark and Ann packed in their suitcase. Encourage students to reread the story on their own and underline the toys to help them with this activity. Reread the story, and underline the toys (i.e., doll, jump rope, games, teddy bear, cars, trucks, planes, blocks, ball) on the transparency as you read them. Read aloud each word under the story, and fill in the bubbles on the transparency next to the toys that were in the story.

3 Give each student a Toy Word Recognition reproducible. Invite volunteers to identify the toy in each box. Say several sentences about each toy. For example, say *My favorite doll is Wendy. My doll has brown hair and a blue dress. I like to play school with my doll.* Tell students to fill in the bubble next to the name of the toy.

4 Display the Toy Word Recognition overhead transparency. Review the correct answers, and have students circle them.

Guided Practice

1 Show the class your ball (favorite toy) from Setting the Stage. Tell the class about the ball and why it is your favorite toy. Invite each student to name his or her favorite toy and give one reason to explain why.

2 Display the Pack Your Toy Suitcase overhead transparency. Invite students to help you write several sentences about where you are travelling, who you are going to see, what toys you will pack, and why they are your favorites.

3 Give each student two Toy Suitcase Pattern reproducibles. Tell students to pretend that they are going on a trip and they may take a suitcase with three to five toys in it. As students decide which favorite toys they want to pack, invite them to create their own suitcase.

4 Show the toy suitcase you made as a sample and explain how students will make their own. Have students cut out both suitcases from the reproducibles, staple the suitcases together along the bottom, and write ____*'s Toy Suitcase* on the front of one of the suitcases. Give each student a piece of string. Tell students to write their name on the name tags, cut them out, and glue them together. Have students hole-punch the name tag and one of the suitcase handles and tie the name tag to the suitcase handle with the string.

5 Invite students to open the suitcase and draw pictures of the toys they will pack on the inside of the back suitcase. Ask them to write the name of each toy they have packed under its picture. If students need help spelling the names of the toys, encourage them to refer to the word bank you recorded in Setting the Stage. Invite students to decorate their suitcase with crayons or stickers.

Independent Practice

1 Invite students to write several sentences about each favorite toy they will pack in their suitcase. Have them include information about where they are travelling, who they are going to see, what toys they will pack, and why these toys are their favorites.

2 Have students revise and edit their rough draft and then use the rubric to evaluate their writing.

Presentation

- Have students **publish** their final drafts on the Pack Your Toy Suitcase reproducibles. Cut them apart and staple them to the inside of the suitcase that folds down as you open it.
- Encourage students to **present** their suitcases to the class along with the real toys that they wrote about.
- **Display** the suitcases in the classroom library.

TEACHING HINTS/EXTENSIONS

- Invite students to hide their favorite toy in a paper bag and bring it to class. Brainstorm several categories of toys such as vehicles, dolls, stuffed animals, and games. Create a graph to illustrate how many toys students brought in each category. Have each student describe his or her toy either verbally or through pantomime, and invite the class to guess what toy is in the bag. For example, a student might describe a toy truck as having four wheels, a steering wheel, and windows, or the student may pretend to drive, holding onto a steering wheel, and then back up making the long beep, beep noise. After students reveal their toy, ask the class which category the toy belongs to, and record it on the graph.
- Show the video *Corduroy* (Paramount) about a toy bear who has many mischievous adventures. Invite students to draw a picture of Corduroy and write about an adventure he has.
- Read aloud the book *Block City* by Robert Louis Stevenson (Puffin), or get the poem on-line at the Poets' Corner Web site at www.poets-corner.org. Invite students to talk about building with blocks. Ask if students have ever built a city with blocks and pretended their sofa was the mountains or the carpet was the sea. Encourage them to build with blocks for a few minutes before going home or during a rainy-day recess. Challenge students to draw a picture of their block city and write several sentences about it.
- Have students complete one or more of these writing prompts in a journal:
  - ✔ Invent a toy. Describe it and convince a parent to buy it for a child.
  - ✔ Invent a toy that takes you places. Describe it and convince someone to take a ride on it.
  - ✔ Think of your favorite toy. Now, change something about it to make it even better. Write how you made your toy even more enjoyable.

Name ____________________ Date ____________________

Favorite Toys

"It is time to pack your suitcase," said Mom. "You are going to visit Grandma. You will need two pairs of shorts, two shirts, shoes, socks, and your favorite toy," added Mom.

Mark and Ann decided to pack their toys first. Ann put her doll and jump rope into the suitcase. Then she added two games and her favorite teddy bear. Mark packed his cars, trucks, and planes. Then he added his bag of blocks and a ball.

"Oh, no," said Mark and Ann. "We have no more room."

"Let's use two suitcases," laughed Mother, "one for your toys and one for your clothes."

Directions: Fill in the bubble next to each toy that Mark and Ann packed.

- ○ blocks
- ○ doll
- ○ book
- ○ kite
- ○ games
- ○ bike
- ○ jump rope
- ○ trucks
- ○ suitcase
- ○ socks
- ○ dog
- ○ teddy bear
- ○ marbles
- ○ Grandma
- ○ planes
- ○ cars
- ○ ball
- ○ scooter

Name ______________________________ Date ______________________

Toy Word Recognition

Directions: Fill in the bubble next to the name of the toy.

○ doll
○ dog
○ door

○ play
○ plant
○ plane

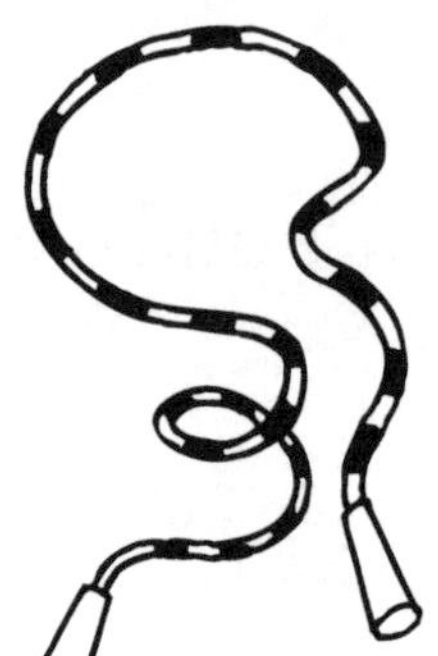

○ jumping jacks
○ jump rope
○ jaguar

○ cart
○ car
○ can

○ ball
○ back
○ balloon

○ blue
○ blocks
○ blow

○ termite
○ teacup
○ teddy bear

○ truck
○ trip
○ trust

Toy Suitcase Pattern

Directions: Cut out two suitcases. Staple the suitcases together at the bottom. Write "_____'s Toy Suitcase" on one suitcase. Write your name on the name tags, cut them out, and glue them together. Hole-punch the name tag and ONE of the suitcase handles, and tie the name tag to the suitcase handle with string. Decorate the outside of your suitcase.

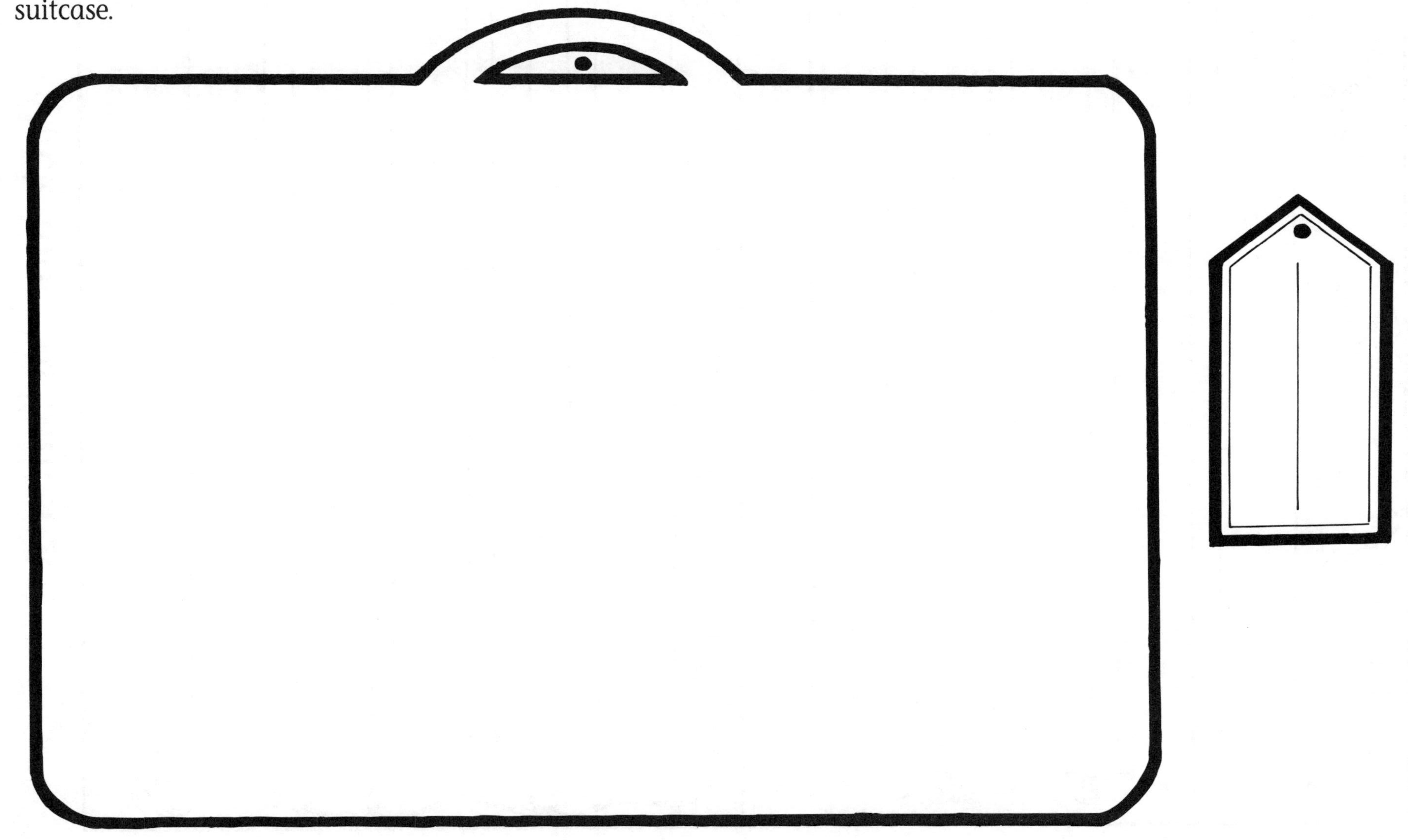

Pack Your Toy Suitcase